AF539671

Pioneering on the Yukon

Anna DeGraf (1839–1930) at Lake La Barge, circa 1897.

Pioneering on the Yukon

1892—1917

by Anna DeGraf

edited by Roger S. Brown

Archon Books 1992

© 1992 Roger S. Brown. All rights reserved.
First published 1992 as an Archon Book, an imprint of.
The Shoe String Press, Inc., North Haven, Connecticut 06473.
Printed in the United States of America

The paper used in this publication meets the minimum requirements of American Natonal Standard for Information Sciences—Permanence of Paper for Printed Library Materials, ANSI Z39.48—1984 ∞

Library of Congress Cataloging-in-Publicaton Data

DeGraf, Anna 1839–1930
Pioneering on the Yukon, 1892–1917
by Anna DeGraf; edited by Roger S. Brown
p. cm.
Summary: Anna DeGraf, an independent pioneer, recounts twenty-five years of adventure in Alaska and the Yukon Territory before, during, and after the Gold Rush.
1. DeGraf, Anna, 1839–1930—Juvenile literature.
2. Frontier and pioneer life—Yukon River Region (Yukon and Alaska)—Juvenile literature. 3. Pioneers—Yukon River Region (Yukon and Alaska)—Biography—Juvenile literature. 4. Women pioneers—Yukon River Region (Yukon and Alaska)—Biography—Juvenile literature.
5. Yukon River Region (Yukon and Alaska)—Gold discoveries—Juvenile literature.
[Degraf, Anna, 1839–1930. 2. Pioneers. 3. Frontier and pioneer life—Yukon River Region (Yukon and Alaska)
4. Yukon River Region (Yukon and Alaska)—Gold discoveries.]
I. Brown, Roger S. II. Title
F1095.Y9D44 1992 979.8'603'092--dc20 92-14808
ISBN 0-208-02362-3

Contents

Foreword

ANNA DEGRAF (1839–1930) MADE TWO GREAT LEAPS, roughly a quarter of a century apart. The first at age twenty-six was from her war-torn Saxon homeland to the New World; the second, at age fifty-three was to the still newer one of the pregold-rush Yukon Territory, and it too was to last a quarter of a century. In between lay a transcontinental leap from New York to the only recently-incorporated Seattle via San Francisco.

Anna DeGraf, then Anna Girndt née Lötsch, made the first leap to follow her husband, a recent immigrant to the U.S. and Civil War veteran, in 1867. By strange coincidence this was the year of Seward's folly, whose parts she was to explore from her late middle age to her old age as a sewing-machine sourdough. The previous and intervening trials and tribulations had evidently steeled her for the hardships and adventures of her Alaskan years. Actually, she had weathered enough drama and trauma for most lifetimes before she reached American shores. For starters, there were the revolution of 1848 and the Seven Weeks War, both of which she witnessed at close range. Then, having lost her first child in infancy, she and her second survived bouts of cholera and a severe storm at sea. After a brief period of relative smooth sailing, her husband lost everything in the panic of 1873, leaving her penniless on the streets of New York with small children.

A new beginning in the West, complete with a name change ended abruptly when her husband was murdered while prospecting near Yakima, Washington. If that weren't traumatic enough, her home and dressmaking business burned to the ground in the great Seattle fire of 1889. She bounced back from these blows as well, only to suffer a badly broken leg and see her son disappear. Down on her luck but characteristically undaunted, she shook the dust of Seattle off her feet and set off for the land of the midnight sun in search of him, armed only with a sewing machine. It is at this point that the narrative contained in the following pages commences. The reader will note that, whereas she never lost sight of her original mission there, and refers to it with fearless hope on the last page, she actually had begun a new life, that of a pioneer. In a way, she had come full circle from her childhood in a mining town to staking claims in the Yukon. From there she helped see her daughter and grandchildren through the San Francisco earthquake among other things, and she remained in the icy North until she heard of the birth of a great-granddaughter in 1917.

We possess the manuscript presented here thanks to the rummaging by two great-grandchildren through her steamer trunk in Oakland in 1982. A subsequent foray into the same trunk by this great-great-grandson produced the leads necessary to flesh out the saga of Anna DeGraf from Saxony to San Francisco. There, at age 85, she wrote her memoirs. Ever exemplifying Saxon industriousness, she was active until age 90 as the wardrobe lady for the Pantages Theater. At 91 she succumbed to pneumonia, never having heard a word from or about the son who sent her over the Chilkoot Pass. Her picture of the

Five Finger Rapids hangs to this day in the home of her death. A pouch of gold nuggets survives her as well.

The memoir exists in undated typescript form, apparently made from the holograph MS (which is not extant). I have refrained from rewriting or "improving" the text. I have, however, silently corrected obvious typographical errors and irregularities made in transcription. The present chapters, and their titles, are editorial; they present the action in five natural blocks, reflecting the narrative structure. The typescript is broken into twenty-nine "chapters" which are given Roman numerals; internal evidence (for which there is no corroboration) suggests the memoir was written in twenty-nine discrete sessions. Where these correspond to natural episodes, or when natural episodes occur, these are indicated editorially by space breaks in the text.

ROGER S. BROWN

1. I made up my mind to go to Juneau

I

It was late in July of the year 1892 that my boy, George, then a young man of twenty-three, said "Good-bye, Mother, I'll see you in fourteen days."

He kissed me and went away. I stood on the front steps of my house in Seattle and watched him as he swung down the street, bag in hand, whistling as he went.

"I'll see you in fourteen days," he called back.

Three weeks passed and he did not return. All inquiries failed to bring news of him. Then a man from Juneau, Alaska, who came to Seattle, called on a young woman friend of mine. She told him of my son's disappearance, and he said he believed a young man of that name had been in Juneau with some other boys. This man wrote to Juneau, and word came back that he was right, the boys had been there.

I made up my mind to go to Juneau.

This was five years before the discovery of the Klondike, but tales about gold being found in the North had made their way into the states and stirred the imaginings of restless and venturesome men. I knew that my boy was filled with a yearning for adventure, and I determined to try to find him. I sold out my business and started on my long journey.

I took my sewing machine along, for I felt that I was

going to an unknown land, where women and their work would be scarce, and it might be necessary for me to earn my living by sewing.

My first intention was to go only to Juneau and look around among the camps near there, for my boy; but that was only the beginning of my travels to and from that Northland.

It would be absurd for me to attempt to cover the story of the progress and development of Alaska and the Yukon Territory during the twenty-five years I was up there. It would take volumes. Rather have I chosen to tell incidents that occurred, and which after all give a more vivid picture of those early days of gold fever, greed, and lawlessness.

I shall never forget my first impressions of Juneau, thirty-three years ago. Then it was not the capital of the territory, but a small frontier town of about one thousand people, most of whom were miners. There was a Mr. Behrends—now a wealthy merchant and banker—who had a little store. Charles Goldstein also had a small store around the corner where he traded with the Indians—quite a different place from the five-story concrete office and store building which now bears his name, and where he has on display many thousand dollars worth of beautiful furs. John Heid was there. He had a good law practice, but was never too busy to listen to my troubles and to give me good advice. But why mention names? The few women who were there, and the men were so kind and helpful to all, that it would be like calling the roll of the town to name them.

There were saloons, a dance hall, and a few general stores on Front Street, and the cabins were scattered on the beach and hillside. At either end of the town was a native village of about two hundred Indians.

Back of the town loomed Mount Juneau, like a great wall, over three thousand feet high. Gold Creek wound its way down through Silver Bow Basin, past Cape Horn and Snowslide Gulch, along the base of Mount Juneau, to Gastineal Channel. Across the Channel, on Douglas, was located the prosperous mining camp of the Treadwell Company.

There was no bank in Juneau, but Mr. Behrends had a safe in his store and miners from a camp called Forty Mile, up on the Yukon, came down and had him put their gold dust in his safe, and went back for more. This was going on for a number of years before the Klondike rush. The miners were keeping it quiet, for they did not want a stampede into that country before they had gotten enough gold dust for themselves. Little did they realize the enormous wealth of that Northland, in minerals, to say nothing of its other great resources.

We did not have steamers from the states very often in

Juneau was a placer mining camp when Anna DeGraf arrived. It was also the seat of government for Alaska beginning about 1884, several years before this photograph was taken.

those days, but when they arrived the whole town—whites, natives, and dogs—gathered on the wharf for the great event. When a boat whistled before making a landing, the malamutes would set up a howl, which was more of a wail than a bark, and if you had not noticed the whistle, you could tell from this chorus that the boat was coming.

The men were rough and ready, and there was little law except as it was enforced with the gun from the hip. Citizens were trying to organize and secure some kind of protection. One of these attempts was the organizing of a fire department, but even primitive man came to the fore here. Jealousy as to who was the best man in this volunteer fire department started the trouble. A personal attack was made in a little local newspaper, and the next day the editor was shot, in the back. There were hardships and privations, of course, but in spite of them we had some good times.

I went out to the different camps to see if I could find my son, but no one could tell me anything about him.

I never had aspirations to become a matchmaker, but somehow I became one. Young men and women came to me in their difficulties and their love affairs—and older men, and dance hall girls, and "squaw men," and squaws themselves. There was romance there—plenty of it.

Girls were very scarce in that country, and if a man wanted to get married he took no chances with time. Even a woman past the heyday of youth was not exempt. It was that way all through Alaska and the Yukon Territory. A girl would come in on a boat and sometimes would be engaged, or even married, within a week. If she was not, it was not on account of lack of proposals. "Squaw men" were very common in those days, and the native Indian women made good wives. I shall tell you more about them later on.

The first marriage I had anything to do with in

Juneau was that of a saloonkeeper and a governess. He was a man in his forties, dignified, good looking, well liked by everybody in the town. He was charitable and grubstaked many a miner. He had been in the saloon business for ten years in Juneau and had made a fortune. The fine young woman came to see me one day and while she was there the saloonkeeper passed and saw her. He must have watched from his saloon down the street to see when she went away, for immediately he came to my door, and remarked:

"That was an attractive young lady who was visiting you."

"Yes", I said, "she is the governess for the two children of the English family on the hill".

"Oh, is that so! I would like to meet her. I want very much to get married".

"You do!" I laughed. It seemed quite sudden, but he did not see anything funny about it. He replied earnestly:

"Yes, I do. You haven't any idea how I long for a home and that lady is the one I want to marry. Will you give me an introduction to her?"

"I will ask her if she wants to get acquainted with you," I said.

"When is she coming to see you again?"

"Maybe tomorrow," I bantered.

"All right, I'll be around."

Sure enough, she did come the following day, and he was not two minutes behind her. He was all dressed up, and succeeded in gaining her consent to go with him to dinner the next evening. He lost no time in his lovemaking, for in such a short time that it made me gasp, they told me of their engagement, and the wedding followed very quickly. I helped to make the wedding gown—of heavy white silk, with a long bridal veil. The groom wore the conventional evening dress which one would expect at a fashionable church wedding in a city, but which was quite a surprise in this little mining town. They were a handsome couple, and were married by the missionary in the little Greek Church in Juneau. I was the matron of honor. There were very few guests at the ceremony, but nearly the whole town was gathered outside the church, for a wedding was quite an event. We had the wedding supper at the hotel and they went to their own home, which he had furnished with the best that could be had. They looked upon me as a sort of fairy godmother, as it was through me they became acquainted, and during the two years I remained in Juneau I was their dinner guest once a week.

Again and again he told me how happy he was, that I had no idea how he had longed for a home. He was very much in love with his wife, who was a good homemaker. So peaceful and harmonious and comfortable was his home that he grew to hate the saloon. Finally he came to me one day, his face wreathed in smiles, and told me he had sold the saloon, and that he was the happiest man in the country. His wife was equally delighted, and the one shadow over their married lives was now removed.

I stayed in Juneau two years, earning my living with my sewing machine. Then a miner and prospector, Joe LaDue, came down from Sixty Mile in the interior, where he had a sawmill on Miller Creek. Some of the lumber which he manufactured was used for sluice boxes by the miners at Forty Mile, which was a good camp then. LaDue told me that a young man by the name of DeGraf had gone through the country with some other boys, and stopped at his sawmill one noon. This made me anxious to get into the interior, and I finally succeeded in finding some people who were going to make the trip. They were a baker and his wife, a man who had been in the Custom Service in Juneau, and a miner they called "Montana" because he came from Montana. I asked to join the party, and we left in July, 1894.

I was one of the first women to enter the Yukon. I made this trip over the Chilkoot Pass and down the Yukon River to Circle City, within a few miles of the Arctic Circle, in my ordinary clothing—a heavy short skirt, blouse and warm jacket, cap and heavy shoes. I took along my feather bed that I had brought from Germany when a girl. That feather bed went in and out of that country with me on seven round trips. I took my sewing machine and had it taken apart, so it could be packed over the Pass.

We went in a small tug boat to what is now Skagway, there being no steamers running then to that place. Skagway was a wilderness. There was one white man and his squaw living there, on a little ranch. Here our things were dumped out on the rocks and we had to get a row boat to take us to Dyea, to go into the country over the Chilkoot Pass. This Pass was used then because, while it was very much steeper and much more difficult to climb, it was a much shorter route into the interior.

We pitched our tents at Dyea and here a pleasant surprise awaited me. A little girl was sitting before a log house; something told me I had seen her before. I stood looking at her, then asked her name. She said, "Herring," which meant nothing to me. I then asked her to take me to her mother, who proved to be a woman I had known years before in Fort Benton, Montana, when she was a little girl. Her little daughter was her exact image. The mother exclaimed when she saw me, "Why, Mrs. DeGraf, for goodness sake, what are you doing up here?" I told her my errand, and she was full of sympathy. She called her husband, who was a pleasant, kind man. He said, "By Jove, this mother must have a horse to take her to Sheep Camp, to help her find her boy." I stayed for supper with them, and we had a fine visit.

The next morning Mr. Herring brought out the horse and I mounted and rode to Sheep Camp. He sent a man along to take the horse back to Dyea. We arrived at Sheep Camp that night. Here we hired some Indians and began packing our goods on the trail. Men could carry 100 pounds, squaws 50, and even the children helped. We paid the packers 15 cents a pound for packing. Father, mother, and the children would all go over the trail with their backs loaded.

Dogs were scarce in that section, and horses were almost unheard of, for the way was so steep and rocky that they could not get over the Pass. So we had to make it on foot, and it was on foot or by boat all the way to Circle City. The trip was hard for me for I still walked with a crutch, as I had broken my leg a few years before and it still gave me trouble. But I was as eager as the rest to get into the interior. I had enough money to hire Indians to pack my provisions, and I felt sure I could get through.

We averaged between twenty and twenty-five miles a day for almost the entire trip. In the morning, the packers would start out and go as far as they could walk, (keeping in mind they had to get back to camp by night), leave their packs covered with canvas, and come back for supper and to spend the night where our tents were. We had two tents; the baker's wife and I slept in one, and the men in the other. We went to bed early, although the nights were almost like day; and were up early in the morning. We kept this up, laying and relaying until everything was out of the tents; then we would carry them along and pitch them where the provisions had been left, and start the same process again. We met very few miners on this trip, in fact, saw scarcely any human beings after leaving Dyea. There were no snakes in that country, nor any thorny bushes called "devil clubs," so we had no fears about going into the thick underbrush to make camp. There were bears, but although we saw a number, they did not molest us.

At Sheep Creek we saw something of the native Indians. Whiskey had already invaded the country, and the Indians must have their "firewater." I saw an old Indian chief sitting on a stump one day, shaking a big bottle vigorously. I asked him what he was doing. He said, "Making hootch." I said, "What is hootch?" He grinned and licked his lips and replied, "Hootch—heap good!" He continued to shake that bottle all day, and when we left, he was still shaking it.

That night eight men arrived from Juneau, packing Whiskey into the Interior. They tried to keep it from the Indians by hiding it in the woods, but the Indians found one keg, and proceeded to celebrate. I stood in the tent and witnessed a most terrible sight. A young Indian woman, with her baby strapped on her back, came out into the open, and her husband, who was drunk, tried to shoot her. She grabbed the gun and broke it over her knee and threw it away; then she went at him with her bare hands. It is literally the truth when I tell you she simply tore the flesh from his face and threw the pieces on the ground. She had the strength and ferocity of a wild beast. It was a sight so surprising and appalling that I had not the power to move, but saw it through. We ran and hid in the woods for we did not know how soon the drunken, fighting Indians might attack us.

Our Indians got some of the whiskey and the result was that they refused to continue packing. So we had to do our own packing from there on, and this made our progress very slow, for the men of our party could not carry as much as the Indian men, and I could only pack about thirty pounds.

From Sheep Camp we entered a canyon, and continued the climb upward to what was called the Scales. Our travel became slower and slower, for the grade was getting very steep, and we had to climb over and around jagged rocks, sometimes jumping from one to another, like mountain goats. From the Scales it was almost perpendicular to the summit, which was 3000 feet above sea level and above timber line. Often I was compelled to thrust out my crutch and one of the party would grasp it and pull me up.

It was sunset when we reached the top, and a wonderful panorama met our eyes. There were seven glaciers in view, and the sun shining on the ice played all the colors of the rainbow. I was so impressed I felt I could never go on. Some of the party were impatient and wanted to push ahead. "Oh, come on," they said, "we don't care about scenery, we want to find gold." I exclaimed aloud, "My God, how beautiful you have made the world!" We camped there all night, and the next morning started over the other side, crossing a glacier in one place. There were deep crevasses in the ice and one mis-step might have sent us to oblivion. I thought, as I gazed about, people do not need to go to Switzerland for magnificent scenery.

I could not walk as fast as the others because of using a crutch, and lingered behind sometimes to admire the wonderful view. One evening I suddenly discovered I was all alone and did not know which way to go. It was getting late. I sat on a rock and listened to the wolves howling. I was afraid to go forward for fear of losing the trail. Then I did what I always do when in doubt. I prayed, "Father, send me some one to show me the way." I did not know where the guide would come from, but I felt sure one would come, and one did. It was not long before I heard a rustling in the bushes, and I started not knowing whether it was a wolf—but presently I saw a little Indian girl coming toward me.

"Do you know where Lake Lindemann is?" I asked.

She made no answer, but stood staring at me. I had a bag of crackers and from it took two and held them out to

The Scales, Chilkoot Pass, 1898.

her. She ate them solemnly and I repeated the question. Again she did not answer, nor could I get a word out of her until I had convinced her that she had eaten all the crackers I had.

"Is Lake Lindemann this way?" I asked, almost in despair, pointing in the direction I felt the lake must be. She smiled shyly and shook her head and pointed in the opposite direction. Then I took her hand and we walked along. She led me up a little hill and I looked over and there saw lights which I knew must be at Lake Lindemann. I turned to thank my little companion, but she had slipped away and I did not see her again. I reached the camp, footsore and weary, about eleven o'clock, and my party were just starting back to look for me.

At Lake Lindemann trouble began. The baker and his wife started to quarrel, and they kept it up the rest of the trip. He was an elderly man and she was young. "Montana" was surly, and the Custom Officer was also disagreeable.

Here we began to travel by water, and we had to have a rowboat, for there were no steamers. Two men had almost completed a boat and we thought it would take us so long to build one for ourselves that we would like to go with them. It was getting late in the season, and we didn't want to get caught in the ice. We asked one of the men, a Dutchman, and he said he was willing, but would have to ask his partner, a Frenchman. I went over to the other and greeted him in French, and asked him if we could go in their boat. He said, "No, *no*, NO—don't want to be bothered with a fam-lee!" We told him we would be no bother, in fact, would do all we could to help them, and added that he might like to make a little money; that we would pay them two hundred dollars to take the five of us in their boat. He said, "No, no, no, don't want no money—don't like the Dutchman nohow." He flew into a rage and grabbed a hammer and pounded their stove in two; sawed the boat in two; and threw half of their pans to the Dutchman, and went off in the woods and left his own half behind.

Then it was up to us to take the Dutchman with us. He furnished us a good deal of amusement along the way. He carried a big gun strapped on his back and kept talking about killing a bear. He would always be telling us about seeing bear tracks, and we would urge him to go out and shoot the bear. One morning he heard a noise in the woods and was sure this was a bear, and ran off with his gun on his back. As he ran along, a little rabbit jumped out of the bushes and ran ahead of him, and he was so frightened he turned and rushed back to camp, without even pulling the trigger.

We camped in the woods near the shore, and the men worked hard for four or five days, whipsawing the lumber and doing everything possible and necessary to complete the boat. When it was finished, we crossed the lake—a trip of only a few hours. Then we portaged our provisions around the head of Lake Bennett, which took a day. When we were ready to start down that lake the next morning, the Custom Officer looked at the sky and said he thought we had better wait another day, and pointed to a few little clouds which he said meant a storm. The others did not believe him and were anxious to go on. The majority rules, so we got our stuff loaded in the boat and started. We had not gone far when the storm came up, and the waves seemed as high as a house. Our little boat floundered and tossed—to get ahead seemed impossible. But the Custom Officer realizing our danger, shouted to the men, "Row, now, damn you! Row for your lives! Remember, we have women on board!"

He made the baker's wife and me lie down in the bottom of the boat and covered us with canvas, and for hours he kept shouting and swearing to "Montana" and the Dutchman to row - row! It was six that night before we could make a landing. We pitched our tents, and dried our clothes by the fire, and after a good night's sleep were up early the next morning and the sun was shining bright.

From Lake Bennett, we passed into a river known as Windy Arm. Here all along the shore were the wrecks of small boats. After three or four hours we entered Lake Marsh. On the shore we saw a big log house, which the men thought must be a storehouse, and they wanted to go that way and stop for some tobacco. But somehow I didn't like the looks of the lonely place. A sudden fear came over me when I thought of landing there. I took from one of my gunny sacks a box of cigars, which I had brought along for such an emergency as this, and passed it around to the men and begged them to be content and go on.

Later on we learned that two miners were crossing the

lake after we did, and as they neared the shore, rowing toward this house, some bad Indians shot from the building. One of the miners was killed outright. The other was wounded. The Indians came out and threw the wounded one into the water, thinking he was dead, and took the blankets and provisions. The man revived and was finally able to reach the shore, when he crawled on his hands and knees through the woods to a cabin and had just strength enough to fall against the door, then fainted. It happened to be the cabin where an English lord was staying. We had met this Englishman and his party at Lake Lindemann while waiting to finish our boat. He was going through the country with six men on a hunting trip. When the wounded miner reached the cabin and had told his story, the white men organized a party, surrounded the Indians in the log house, and captured them and turned them over to the authorities at Dawson.

We then neared Miles Canyon, passing just before we got there a dangerous place called the Devil's Hole. It is a whirlpool almost enclosed by high, jagged rocks, and the current pulls swiftly that way. Miles Canyon seemed as deep and dark as a dungeon, with high dark walls, and a narrow passage through which the waters whirled at a dizzy rate. You have no idea what a sight it is, unless you have been there yourself, and words fail me in trying to describe it. We did not dare enter the canyon with our heavily loaded row boat, so packed our things four miles around. One of the men in our party lay down flat in the bottom of the boat, and waving his hand, cried to us,

"Here goes nothing!"

and went through the canyon. His boat shot through that boiling, seething, roaring water, and landed him three miles below. While we were there, another boat-load of people came through and upset, and we threw them a rope and fished them out. They camped with us there for a day and a night.

We got our boat and stuff across the river at Miles Canyon and neared the White Horse Rapids, but when the water became too dangerous, the Custom Officer stood in the bow of the boat and threw a rope into a tree on shore, and fortunately, it caught and held. We were swung around and made a landing. We portaged our boat around the rapids, which were a wonderful sight—the water dashing up in white foam. We then entered Lake LaBarge. It was a day's travel down this great body of water, and a beautiful trip we had.

There were all kinds of wild flowers in great quantities, beautiful in color and most fragrant. The masses of wild roses I shall never forget—the air was heavy with their perfume. Then there were loads of berries along the shores. We camped at the end of the lake for a day and it was then I discovered that the finest blueberries I have ever tasted grew in the Yukon Territory. They made great patches of blue among the flowers, and at that time they were so ripe they would fall in showers at a slight shake of the bush. I gathered a panful of them, and that night we had blueberry sauce, and the next day we had blueberry pie. Did anything ever taste better? And there were ripe raspberries and strawberries, which were most delicious. It was a wonderful change from our regular food, and we felt we had a great treat. It was all so beautiful up there—the air was so clear and fresh, the sun so bright, the scenery so grand—I felt as if I could stay there forever; but my anxiety about my boy spurred me on.

Leaving the chain of lakes, we entered the headwaters of the Yukon and shot through one of the channels of Five Fingers like lightning. Here giant rocks stuck high above the waters. Like great fingers. The river was full of cascades, whirlpools and rocks and it was difficult to get our light craft through in safety. Along the way the scenery was most fascinating and varied. Sometimes the high mountains were near at hand, again they were in the distance. The river turned and twisted and some places there were bars and islands. At one place the banks were evenly terraced as though planned by a landscape artist. We wound about for miles and miles and these beautiful wooded banks rose in terraces above the water. Then we entered the broader waters of this mighty river, where the shores widened out.

At Fort Selkirk we found a missionary of the English Church, who made us very welcome. He had labored there among the Indians for many years. He had a fine garden in summer, from which he filled his cellar with vegetables to carry him over the long winter. He took us

The Clifford Sifton negotiates Miles Canyon near White Horse Rapids, summer 1900, after "regular" boat service was established.

down into this cellar and showed us his store of vegetables. There were potatoes, cabbages—the largest and finest, and with a flavor I have never known to be equalled—turnips, beets, celery. He gave us a good dinner of these green things and we felt that we had dined sumptuously. We were sorry to leave this good man—and his store of fresh vegetables.

On and on we went, past the place where Dawson was, three years later, to become a flourishing city and one of the richest mining camps of the Northland. Then it was a wilderness. As we rowed along, I said to the men, "Why don't you stop and prospect along here? This country looks good to me." They said, "Awh, we haven't time, we want to get down to the camp where there is gold,"—meaning Circle City, which was the newest camp at that time.

Then we reached a place called Sixty Mile, where Joe LaDue had his sawmill on Miller Creek. He was the one who had told me in Juneau about a boy named DeGraf being at his place. On our arrival, I inquired eagerly about my boy. The squaw, who was the only one at home, told me it was true, that the boys had been there, but she couldn't tell me whether they had gone down the Yukon, or up the Yukon.

Heartsick, but still hopeful, I wanted to get to Circle City, thinking my boy might be in this new camp. We stopped at Forty Mile for one day, and made inquiries, and about two days later reached Circle City. We landed in a heavy snowstorm, the last of October. The flakes of snow were the largest I have ever seen, and dry like feathers. We had encountered some ice coming down the Yukon, which added to our troubles, and we were fortunate in reaching our destination when we did, for the river froze over the next day. This was in 1894.

The coming of any one to Circle City, in the far North, was an event, especially when it was some one from the great world outside, and as we neared the shore the whole place turned out to greet us. Our arrival swelled the number of white women in the camp from six to eight. There were about two dozen Indian women and some Indian men, and between six and seven hundred miners, who had come in from the creeks for the winter.

Circle City was a strange looking place. Here the Yukon River was very wide and the town of log cabins stretched two miles up and down the river. The street facing the river had buildings only on one side: there were saloons aplenty, a few stores, the largest one being a two-story log store of the Northern Commercial Company. My cabin was on Second Avenue, so-called, almost directly behind the Company store.

Two of the white women kept a little restaurant, and I stayed with them until I could get rested and find work. Work was not long in coming, for the next day two miners, who had seen me land, came and asked me to take care of a sick girl. I was glad to do it, and in three weeks had her well. For this I received $300.00. I was paid in gold dust, which seemed very strange. It was weighted out on some little scales and handed to me in a leather bag which I afterwards learned to call a "poke". An ounce of dust represented from fifteen to seventeen dollars.

Then I set up my sewing machine and began to work for the Northern Commercial Company, and the manager, Mr. McQuesten, gave me some scales of my own to measure out the gold dust I received for my work. I made tents and shirts and did other sewing for the company. I also did sewing for the few white women in the camp, and for some of the miners. When they came to pay me I would tell them to measure out the right amount of gold dust, and they always gave good measure.

This Mr. McQuesten was called the "Father of the Country," and a fine man he was. He had been in the interior many years, had married a native woman, and they had a nice family of nine children at that time. Their ninth child was born in a tent before my cabin door, and it was the most surprising incident you could imagine.

One day I left my cabin and ran over to the company store. After making my purchase I stood and chatted with acquaintances a few minutes, but could not have been gone from my place an hour. As I neared my cabin again, I noticed a small tent had been set up immediately in front of the door. I hesitated, not knowing just what was going on—although one could look for almost anything to happen in that country! In answer to my call, "Who's there?" Mrs. McQuesten came out of the tent, smiling broadly, and carrying something in her apron.

"What is it?" I asked—"What is the matter?"

"Nothing the matter," she replied, "I have baby girl," and to my astonishment she unfolded her apron and showed me a newly-born naked baby.

"But why didn't you go into the cabin?—my door was open."

"Oh, no, Indian babies must always be born in the fresh air."

The two Indian women who were with her, took down the tent, put it on their backs and marched off with Mrs. McQuesten, still carrying the baby in her apron.

A number of Indian women were married to white men, and I must say they were good, peaceable, industrious women, who did all they could to make their white husbands comfortable. The Indians had a large village a mile from Circle, and here the white men purchased wives from the chief of the tribe, giving provisions and blankets in exchange. Some of the young girls were sold when they were twelve years old, and many of them had sweet faces.

I remember one wedding that took place shortly after my arrival. A young miner bought an Indian girl and took her home to his cabin. That night the whole camp turned out to serenade them. The noise was terrific and continued until the groom finally came to the door, and said,

"Well, boys, what do you want?"—thinking the reply would be, "All we can drink." But not so. This native girl was exceptionally pretty and there had been some contest for her hand, especially on the part of one young miner, who called out, "Give me back my chicken you stole!"

The men up there who had married squaws appeared satisfied with their domestic arrangements. There seemed to be an attraction about these native women that the men could not resist, and until the dance-hall girls came in, the men as a rule were faithful and fond of their wives and children. I knew of one Englishman who was married to an Indian woman. A few years later I heard that through the death of an elder brother he had come into the family estate. He felt that he could not take his wife to England with him, so rather than leave her he gave up his inheritance.

I got to know most of the Indians there very well. The women made mukluks, and moccasins, which they beaded in beautiful designs. I have been in their cabins, where they sit on the floor in a circle, one candle in the center, and their fingers flying as they worked and chatted away.

It was hard to get the commonest kind of labor done at Circle City. White men did not want to saw wood or build cabins; they wanted only to look for gold, so it was difficult for me to get wood sawed. But there was a young Indian named Charlie who was willing to do odd-jobs for me. When he came in the winter time it was so bitter cold—sixty to seventy below zero—that he could work only a few minutes outdoors, then had to come in and get warm. I limbered him up by giving him a cup of hot coffee. He would work a while, then come in to thaw out and get a cup of coffee, and go at his wood sawing again. That Indian was always cold!

The day before Christmas, the first winter I was there, he was sawing wood for me and when he was about to leave I called him in and asked him about his family. He said he had a wife and baby boy. I gave him some bits of ribbon and lace, and a box of candy which my daughter had given me before I left Juneau and which I had tossed on a shelf when I unpacked my belongings on moving into the cabin at Circle. Charlie had never seen candy and was as delighted as a child when he tasted it. He said he could give it to his baby. I told him the things were Christmas presents for his wife and baby.

"What is Christmas?" he asked.

Then I told him about the Christ child, the little babe, and about the Wise Men from the East bringing Him gifts, and explained that was why people gave one another gifts on His birthday. Charlie thought about it a minute and then said, "Me sabe—me never knew—me tell wife." Later he told me his wife and baby clapped their hands for joy, and that he had told the wife the reason for Christmas. One thing about the Indians: do them a good turn and they never forget it, but return it with more added for good measure. Charlie was no exception.

Later in the winter, when no one in the camp had fresh meat for a long time, the weather moderated and some of the Indians went hunting. They brought home a moose and divided it amongst themselves. That night about twelve o'clock Charlie knocked at my door.

"Why Charlie," I cried in surprise, "what do you want this time of night?"

"Open door, quick!"

I let him in, and he laid down a big piece of moose meat.

"You give me candy, you give me presents for wife and baby—you tell me story of Christ baby: I bring you meat for winter. Cook at night so white man won't smell, for he not get any."

I worked hard all winter, hoping to be able to go outside—to the States—in the Spring. There was little to do but work. I was homesick and lonely, and two celebrations cheered me up quite a bit. There was a wedding on Christmas Eve. One of the friends who kept the restaurant and with whom I stayed when I first arrived, married a saloonkeeper. I made the wedding gown, and was invited to the festivities, and we had a happy time. They were married in due form and the papers had to be sent to Juneau in the Spring to be recorded.

But the Pioneer's Dance, given on New Year's night was something I shall always remember. About eight hundred men were wintering in Circle; there were eight white women, and about thirty squaws who had married white men. There were no social distinctions; most of the white folks knew the squaws were good women, and the fact that the squaws were going to the dance was all right with everybody except one white woman. She made quite a fuss about it, and said that if the squaws went to the dance, she would not go. The men talked it over and finally told her that the squaws had been good wives and had taken care of them when they were sick, and they were not going to leave them out; that if she didn't want to go to the dance she could stay home, for the squaws were going. She didn't go.

Everybody in town knew I had dressed the Christmas bride, so the squaw-men came and asked me to fix up their wives for the dance. They told me to go to the store and get anything I needed and they would pay the bills. I bought the best materials I could find. I had to begin at the very foundation with the squaws, so the first thing they had to do was take a bath. As chance would have it, a bundle of corsets had been sent in to the store by mistake from the States, and I bought them. Some of the Indian women were delighted—and some horrified! They were like children, and giggled and bothered me with questions about what they were going to wear. Some of them had silks and velvets, but there was not enough of these materials to go around, so the rest had to wear gingham dresses—but they were fixed up with bits of trimming and lace I had brought from the States, and they were happy, too. I happened to have a small pot of rouge and some face powder, and a few artificial flowers, and I fixed up the squaws—curled and arranged their hair, and so on, until their own husbands hardly knew them—and the squaws almost died of pride and joy.

A few of the most prominent citizens drew lots for the privilege of taking the white women to the dance. My lot fell to Judge Metlock, who came for me with a dog team, and bundled me up with big fur robes. It was an extremely cold night, somewhere around seventy below. Every time the door of the ballroom was opened, a great puff of frosty air blew in like a cloud of smoke.

The dance was given in the Opera House, the one place of entertainment. The floor was fairly smooth. First the tables were set for the banquet—two long ones—and afterwards they were removed and the chairs pushed back against the wall to make room for dancing. There was a dressing room for the women and one for the men. In the latter was a little piece of looking glass, and the men almost had a fight to hold their places in front of it. They pushed and dug their elbows into each other. And when they emerged—what a sight! The squaws didn't have anything on them!

Some of the men wore overalls, some had on fur coats and mukluks, others came in makinaw shirts and trousers tucked in boots. But there were two honest-to-goodness dress suits there. No one knew where they came from, except the wearers, and they wouldn't tell. The suits did not fit, and looked too funny for words. One of these men was very tall and had on a coat so small that the cuffs of the sleeves hit him about halfway between wrist and elbow; and the trousers were way above his ankles, but he wore mukluks to cover the interval. The other dress suit hero was "Buckskin" Miller. He was a small man, and his swallow-tail almost touched the floor. His clothes were so big they bagged all over. He wore a high white collar with stiff points that jabbed his chin if he turned his head, consequently he carried his head very stiff and looked straight ahead. A red bandana for a necktie completed his costume. But do you think those men would exchange dress suits?—not much! Buckskin Miller pranced around like a little bantam rooster. He positively knew he was the swellest dressed man at that dance.

And that reminds me to tell you how he got his name. He had been in the Cassiar country before coming to Circle City, and had lost his way on the trail. His provisions gave out, and the only thing that kept him from starving was his buckskin shirt. He cut pieces from the shirt, shredded them fine with his knife, and fried them in the grease of his one candle. He had to eat quite a lot of his shirt and all of his candle before he found his way on the trail again. And so the name "Buckskin" Miller stuck to him.

Well, I tell you, we had a wonderful banquet! The tables were loaded with the best the camp afforded. Probably the greatest treat was the fresh potatoes—not the evaporated kind that we ordinarily had. These fresh potatoes had been brought in before the river froze over, and were carefully taken care of so as not to freeze. We had fresh cabbage too, and moose meat roasted, blueberry sauce that had been preserved in old bottles—and among other things a keg of beer. We sat at the table two hours, and there were songs and speeches. The ladies, white and natives, were toasted, and we had a happy time. Of course, only a comparatively small number were at the banquet, for no hall in the town was big enough to seat all the miners who attended the dance.

An orchestra of fourteen volunteer musicians had

been rounded up, and these with their cornets, violins, trombones, banjos, and other instruments, made pretty good music. The quadrilles were "called off" in old fashioned, backwoods style.

That day while I was dressing the squaws and arranging their hair, I ran out of hairpins and went over to the store for more. On the way I met a man who stopped me and shook hands and said I was the first white woman he had seen in fifteen years. It may have seemed that long to him, but I think he stretched the time a bit! Anyway, he was so happy to see a white woman. He said he had come in to town for the dance, and added, "God bless you! will you give me a dance this evening?" His clothes were worn and soiled, he was bent over, and his face was covered with whiskers, and he did not look attractive: but I said I would give him a dance if I could arrange it. That evening a nice looking, straight, clean-shaven young man came up and claimed the dance he said I had promised him. I could not believe that this was the same man I had talked with that afternoon in the street so great was the transformation!

There were so many more men than women at the party that we could dance only once around the hall with a partner, when some one else would come up and claim us for the next round. Men danced with each other when they had no women partners, and those who could not dance stood around the edge of the hall and enjoyed watching the others. And the squaws—how they dance! The white men had taught them, and the younger women were graceful dancers—and most of them were young girls.

We had quadrilles and waltzes, then a polka mazurka was announced. None of them could dance it except one man and myself. The orchestra struck up and we danced round and round the hall, while the others looked on, and gave us a hearty hand-clap when we had finished.

I had worked so hard during the day getting all those squaws ready for the dance, that when midnight came I was very tired and wanted to go home, so another woman and I tried to slip away, but some of the men came out and begged us to stay. So we went back, and we had coffee and cake at midnight. We had some songs, and we danced until morning. Then we started again to leave, and the men begged us to stay. "Oh, please, don't go" they implored; "we won't have another party like this for a year: we are having such a good time, and if the ladies will only stay we will get breakfast and then you will all feel rested." So we stayed on, and they cooked breakfast for us, and we danced until almost noon. Then we were taken home in the dogsleds, and the entire town was absolutely dead to the world the rest of that day and all the following day.

The people in this camp were kind and neighborly as a rule, and all went well, except when the men got drunk. I was molested only a few times.

One summer evening I was sitting in my cabin finishing a tent for the Company. My sewing machine was near the window, and altho it was quite late, it was very light so that I could see to sew without lighting my coal-oil lamp. There was a little wooden bench by the door upon which my visitors sat. In response to a knock, I said, "Come in"—and went on sewing, thinking it was some one from the Company store to get the tent; but it proved to be a husky six-footer, whom I had never seen before. He told me he had come for his tent. I said,

"This tent belongs to the Company." He insisted it was his. I said, "It belongs to the Company, and I shall not deliver it to a stranger."

"But it is mine" he said more emphatically.

"That makes no difference," I said; "you sit there on the bench until it is finished, then you can carry it to the Company store, and I will go with you."

He did not sit down, but came over and grabbed me by the shoulders. I said, very positively, "You go and sit down on that bench until I finish this tent for the Company." He did go back, but before he sat down, he locked the door and put the key in his pocket. My heart was in my mouth, but I pretended not to see what he had done. All the time he sat there I could feel him staring at me, but I sewed and thought, racking my brain for a way to make him open the door. Finally I looked at my woodbox, luckily it was empty.

I jumped up and said, "Oh, I must get some wood!" speaking as naturally as I could. "Will you help me bring it in, so I can finish the tent for the Company?" I went over to the door and appeared surprised to find it locked, and said that if I didn't have some wood to keep up my fire I could not finish the tent for the Company, and asked him to open the door. He stood glaring at me, then finally unlocked the door. We went out to my woodpile, and when he stooped to pick up some wood, I grabbed a heavy stick and as he straightened up I struck him across the face with all my might. The roar of rage he gave brought men from the neighboring cabins; first they stuck their heads out of the door, then came over to see what was going on. I shouted to them, "Boys, come out here, and look at the man who barred my door, and see what he got for it." Then the men crowded around, but this miner pushed his way through them and disappeared, swearing he would get even with me. I said to him, "Now, you go back to the creek and tell the miners that the dressmaker gave you a licking for not behaving yourself."

The next morning I went over and told the Company manager my troubles. I said, "This is a pretty howdy-do; if a woman cannot make an honest living in this town I am going to write on to Washington and get the soldiers." He handed me a six-shooter and gave me permission to use it if I was ever molested again. He begged me not to write to Washington, and said everything would be all right. Little did I think I should have cause to use the gun soon, but it was only a few nights afterward that I was wakened by terrible screams, and I heard some one running to my cabin.

"What is it?" I called.

"For God's sake, open the door, quick!" called a woman's voice. I opened the door, and there stood the only dance-hall girl in the camp at that time.

"Let me in, quick, and shut the door! They are after me" she cried; "don't let them get me!" She was so cold and frightened that I had to pull her in the room. She told me that six men had entered her cabin and started a "rough house" and because she protested, they set her on her cookstove, which was red hot, and as a result she was painfully burned and was groaning and suffering terribly. I put her in my bed and made her as comfortable as I could, and told her to be quiet; turned out the light, stood with my six-shooter, and waited. I rather doubted that they would follow her, but, sure enough, I heard them coming—like a pack of wolves! They talked a while outside, then a knock came on my door. I was so frightened I could not answer at first, but when they knocked again, I said,

"Who's there?"

"We want that woman in your cabin," they called through the door. "We won't bother you if you let us have her."

"You won't get her, as long as I am in here with my gun," I shouted back.

"Open this door" was their angry demand.

"I will not open the door, and I will shoot the first man that comes in here."

They commenced to shake the door back and forth. I was terrified, expected every moment they would break it down. I pointed my gun at the door and pulled the trigger, and counted aloud—"One!-two!-three!"—and fired three times through the door, and then I heard them run. In a few seconds I opened my door and saw the Company watchman running toward my cabin. I told him what had happened and he stood guard at the cabin while I ran to tell the manager—to whom I always appealed in time of trouble.

The next day I agitated the question of lawlessness vigorously. The Company manager got the miners together in a mass meeting and decided to put up signs all over the camp, warning any one who tried to do any crooked work that he would be run out of the camp and left to starve. The miners feared that almost more than anything else—for in that country, in the winter time, it meant death from starvation or cold.

But those six big fellows were not routed by a woman without trying somehow to get even. This same woman whom I had befriended came running to my cabin one evening, and said,

"If you have any money in your cabin, hide it. I overheard some of those fellows that you got ahead of, talking together and they are planning to come and beat you and take your money late tonight."

"They'll find very little," I said, "but I am glad you warned me; I'll be ready for them."

With that I took what little gold dust I had and put it in the Company's safe and told the manager what the woman had said. One of the men who had a badge of authority from the Northern Commercial Company came and hid himself behind a curtain in my cabin, and we waited. It was sometime after midnight when a knock came on my door, and when I opened it, I saw two men. One of them said,

"Can you change some money for us?"

"No, you know there is very little money in this country. I have scales, and you can weigh your gold dust if you want to," I said.

'We want to see your dust," he growled, and with that he pushed me aside and started to hunt around the cabin, while his companion watched me. Then the officer stepped out from behind the curtain. In a jiffy their hands were above their heads, and the officer marched them out of my cabin, and the balance of the night they were kept in another cabin, under guard, and the next day they were ordered to leave the camp. After that I was never bothered again. The whole town knew those signs meant business.

The first winter I was in Circle City, flour was $125 a sack and other provisions were very high. Meat was scarce; when I had any I kept it on top of my cabin, where it would freeze, and the dogs could not get to it. When I wanted some meat, I would bring the frozen chunk down from the roof, chop off a piece with the axe, let it thaw out in water, and fry it. We always treated moose meat in this way, and it was very palatable. In summer, I had an ice box under my cabin merely by taking out a board of the floor and setting a box underneath, for ice did not thaw under the cabin; there was ice under there all the year round.

After the first winter there, I was hungry for fresh vegetables, and as my cabin had a mud roof, here was my opportunity! I could not plant anything in the ground around the cabin, for the dogs would have torn up a garden. I had some seeds I brought from Juneau, and I planted them on my roof, and had a fine garden. There were onions, radishes, lettuce, and some celery. Vegetables grew fast in that country, with twenty-four hours of light each day, for three months. The Hanging Gardens of Babylon, though quite different, could not have afforded any more joy to the ancients than my own little roof-garden on the Yukon did to me!

We had a variety of good things to eat in the summertime. The Indians brought in salmon. We had mountain sheep, venison and moose, caribou and bear meat. Sugar, molasses, flour and such staples had to be brought in from "below"—the States. We ate a great deal of molasses, on hot cakes, which were usually called "sour dough" cakes in the north. The Custom Officer used to wake us every morning on the trail by singing a little song of his own, which, though not elegant, was an effective substitute for an alarm clock to get us up for breakfast. It ran

"Slop cakes in the morning,
And whiskey when I'm dry—
We are sailing down the Yukon
And never, never die!"

The first winter was a terrible one—seventy below zero a good deal of the time. Most of the miners came in from the creeks to wait until they could work their claims again in the Spring. They did not take care of themselves. They lived principally on bacon and beans, and scurvy broke out among them and several died.

Mrs. Healy, the wife of the groceryman, was a most charitable, lovely woman. Many a time she had me go with her to take things to the sick men. She would say, "My goodness! we must do something for these poor men! They are so far away from their families and friends, and are lonely!" But it was too late to do anything in some cases. In spite of all their gold dust, they had to leave it. When the end came, they were put into wooden boxes; but the ground was so hard that they could not be buried. Men were detailed to take turns guarding the boxes to keep the wolves away, until the springtime came and graves could be dug.

The Snow family were a great comfort and blessing to that camp, especially in the winter. The father and mother were very musical and had been actors in the States. Their little boy and girl showed decided musical talent and acted well in the little one-act plays that were given at the Opera House. Usually the Snows would arrange a little play, some music, then we would dance, and go home cheered and happy. Mr. Snow had a rich baritone voice, and I shall never forget the way he sang "Kathleen Mavourneen".

I was glad when the snow began to melt. Then the ice broke up in the Yukon River. I had traveled something like two thousand miles, and had heard of my boy only twice, and then that he had gone to some other place. I had not had any news from my daughter since the summer before, when I left Juneau, for she did not know where to address me. I was quite discouraged and watched anxiously for the boat to come and take me down the Yukon on my journey to the States, but here again I was doomed to disappointment. Every summer a government boat would come from Seattle to St. Michael at the mouth of the Yukon River. There the Company boat would meet it and take over the supplies for the camps along the river. But that summer it did not arrive at Circle City until late in August—too late to get back to St. Michael in time to connect with the government boat returning to the States. Men could get out of the country by poling up the Yukon, but women could not go that way. It was a harder and slower trip than we had made coming down the river. So I was forced to spend another winter there. I felt as though I was locked up in Siberia, and the key lost. But I made the best of it—I didn't want to mope around and make myself disagreeable to everybody.

I had not been able to send my daughter any word for almost a year and was delighted when I heard that a Jewish gambler called "Goldie" was going up the river on the ice, over the Pass and out to the States by way of Skagway. So I went to see if he would take some letters for me. He said he would, and that the charge was $1 per letter. That made $3 for one letter to my daughter, and two others to friends. Goldie said he would have to wear a mask to protect his face from cutting winds, and I offered to make it. I had some pieces of satin which I quilted and made the mask soft and warm. I took it with my letters to where Goldie was preparing to leave. I handed him the three letters and $3, and the mask, and told him I would have to charge him $5 for it. So he had to hand back my three dollars (in gold dust) and two more, and those who stood by and saw the transaction set up a shout and joked him. This story was told all over Circle City, and later in Dawson, wherever "Goldie" put in an appearance, some one would be sure to remember to tell the story about how the dressmaker in Circle got ahead of the Jew.

Indeed, Goldie returned to Circle in the spring with a stock of goods, and paid me the compliment of asking me to take charge, and sell it for him, but I declined as I was expecting to go back to the States.

The summer of 1895 some dance hall girls came down the Yukon River, and then the squaw men began to treat their wives badly. They spent all their money on the dance hall girls and neglected the women who had been faithful to them and worked so hard for their comfort, in some cases for years. One instance of this was in a cabin next to mine.

A white man had married a squaw and they had five children. She was an industrious, good woman, and the children were nice little things. He did freighting to the claims, fifty and sixty miles away on the creeks, and made lots of money. He had the only two horses in Circle City—which had been brought up the river by way of St. Michael, as no horses could be brought over the Passes and down the Yukon.

One night I heard a terrible rumpus next door—

chairs knocking against tables and things smashing generally; then a woman screamed. I jumped out of bed, threw something around me, and ran over. The door was not barred so I opened it and entered. The man had a chair lifted above his head and was about to bring it down on the woman, when I yelled at him,

"You put that chair down, and do it quick!"

He was startled and enraged, and growled, "Don't you interfere here. What business is this of yours?" I said,

"I will interfere. You stop abusing that woman or I'll go over to the Company and report you."

Evidently he remembered what happened to the other men when they didn't behave, so he put down the chair. After things got quiet and I felt the man had worn out his anger, I went home. The next day the squaw told me that she and the children had had nothing to eat for two days; that when she asked her husband for money to buy food, he would fly into a rage and begin to beat her and spend his money at the dance hall.

This neighbor of mine also had some dogs to help in hauling to the camps. He whipped the dogs and made them stay out in the storm when it was sixty to seventy below zero. Many a night have I opened the storm door to the little entry of my cabin and laid gunny sacks on the floor for the dogs to sleep on. I always got up early the next morning and let them out before their master found out about it; and those poor dogs would lick my hands to show their gratitude. One time when the front door into my cabin was open and I stepped out the back door for a second, the whole bunch—eight big malamutes—rushed in and grabbed a sheepskin rug that was in front of the stove, and tore it to pieces and were devouring the last bits of it when I came back into the room.

When the dance hall girls came in, I had a good deal of work to do. I continued to sew for the Company during the daytime, and at night made clothes for the girls. But up there, in summer, when it was light day and night, it wasn't hard to keep awake. On Sundays I always rested and usually took a long walk if the weather permitted, for I wanted to see as much of the country as I could. The hills back of the town were wooded, and it was all so wild and interesting. The wild flowers and berries were so plentiful; the air was warm and delightful during the day; but it was cool at night and I had to keep a fire going when I sewed late. And how lovely those nights were!

That summer I was working very late one night. I wanted to get some wood, and as I stepped out the door I saw a wonderful sight—the midnight sun! It was the longest day of the year, and the sun was blood red and seemed about five times as big as I had ever seen it before. I took a chair outdoors and sat and watched this great fiery ball go down, down, until there was only a tiny piece left—then the scene changed. The birds began to twitter, the wild creatures in the woods began to make noises; the sun came up higher and higher—and now it was as golden as anything you could imagine, and the full round morning sun flooded everything with sunshine. It was indeed a most glorious sight.

In winter too, the sights were marvelous. The stars seemed so big and bright, and so near. When the moon shone, it was almost like day; the snow covered up the unsightly objects, and with the floods of moonlight streaming down on the little snow-covered cabins, the field of ice on the Yukon, and the frost crystals sparkling on the trees—it was a beautiful picture. But, oh, so cold!

One winter's night another woman and I were returning from the Opera House, where the Snow Family had given us a delightful entertainment. Something flashed across the sky and startled me, with its beauty and wonder. I heard a hissing sound. It was a great light of many colors, flashing back and forth over the sky, and it seemed to come down around me, like lightning. Many times have I seen the Northern Lights in that country, but nowhere else were they so beautiful and marvelous as in Circle City.

I had not been in Circle City very long before I noticed a lot of half-breed children running around the streets, and this disturbed me. One day as I stood talking with some women on the street, I said, "These children ought to be in school instead of roaming around like stray sheep!"

They agreed, but they said, "How can we get a school?"

"The quickest way is to give a dance," I replied, "and bake cakes and sell them." Right there in the street, plans were made. Mrs. Healy said we could use their grocery store for the dance. We went around at once and solicited cakes from the baker and all the women in the place. We invited the miners and told them why we were giving the dance, and they all turned out. The baker contributed a huge cake in the form of a pyramid. This one was auctioned off, and the richest young miner in the camp won it. He gave it back, and three times it was auctioned and each time he was the lucky one. It brought $300. Other cakes were then auctioned, and we raised quite a sum of money—enough to build a schoolhouse. A number of men volunteered to put up the building. We wrote to Washington and asked that a teacher be sent. When she arrived the following summer, everything was ready. We felt it was the best thing that ever happened to Circle City. She was a lovely young woman, well educated, and of fine character, and was glad to do all she could for the children. But conditions were very raw and crude and quite different from those she had left, and she was homesick. But she was brave and stuck it out, and was still there when I left for the States the following summer.

The school was an influence for good to the grown-ups as well as the children. That was years before the days of phonographs, moving pictures, or the radio. We had no telegraphic communication with the outside world, no newspapers, no magazines and few books, and for nine months of the year no letters.

Finally the second summer came, and the Company boat arrived from St. Michael and brought provisions and took passengers back to connect at St. Michael with the boat for the States. I was good and ready to go, after two long, hard, dark winters near the Arctic Circle. I sold my sewing machine to a squaw for $100. It was a time of great rejoicing for those who were leaving for the great world outside. Among the passengers were forty miners who were going out with their clean-ups. The claims around Circle were rich. The miners would come to town with their pokes of gold dust and nuggets, and some of them poured out their wealth at the saloons and dance hall as though it was so much sand from the sea. Others saved their gold. One little Englishman who was on the boat made ten thousand dollars out of his claim, and there were dozens who got that much and more out of small holes in the ground.

On our journey down the Yukon, we crossed the Arctic Circle, and had a wonderful trip. At a Russian Mission we stopped a whole day while some of the machinery of the boat was repaired. The Indians here were quite different from any others I had ever seen. Their hair was wild and bushy and stood straight out from the head. Both men and women wore big brass rings in their noses and ears, and their faces were tattooed. They looked quite fierce and savage, but really were not, as I had occasion to find out.

While the boat was being repaired, I went out on deck to sit in the sunshine, taking some sewing. It was not long before I noticed a group of squaws on the shore motioning and jabbering; they were evidently excited about something. Pretty soon one of them came up the gang-plank and stood in front of me. I held my needle toward her. She grinned and turned and motioned to the others on shore, and they came aboard. I went to my cabin and got some bright pieces of cloth and ribbons, and some leftovers of sugar, crackers, tea, and the like, which I had brought from Circle, and gave these to the women. The children who were with them grabbed the sugar and ate it

Children and puppies somehow survive without formal schooling. The identity of the boy is unknown, but the picture was later found in Anna DeGraf's treasure trunk, along with a poke of gold nuggets.

greedily. One of the Indian men tasted the tea and chewed it, and ran away with the package into the woods. Evidently he thought it was tobacco and had no intention of sharing it with the others.

Later in the day, the Indian women came back and gave me three lovely mink skins, and by motioning made me understand that they wanted me to accept them because of what I had given them. I offered to pay for the skins, but they refused to accept anything. One of them had around her neck a piece of bright red ribbon which was among the things I had given them and doubtless she felt very much dressed up.

After some days on the steamer—lazy, restful days spent on deck as we steamed down the ever widening, mighty river—we reached St. Michael and spent several days here. Some of us attended services at the little Greek Church on Sunday. The Indians had quite a parade on their way to church, beating drums and making a noise on their native instruments which they probably thought was music. The service was in Russian, which we could not understand; but it was an interesting sight, and we were glad to know about the work that the missionary was doing for the natives.

We did not transfer to the government steamer at a wharf, but had to go out in a small boat, and up a rope ladder, and over the side of the Seattle-bound boat, in a heavy, rough sea, which was quite an exciting experience. The trip from St. Michael was terrible and took six weeks. The weather was very stormy, the waves seemed mountain high, and tossed our boat about like a chip. The captain proceeded with great caution as he said he did not want to risk the lives of the passengers. Practically all on board, except the captain and some of the crew, were seasick from the first, and kept to their berths.

There was an Irish girl in the berth above mine, who

The Russian Greek-Catholic church at St. Michael's, Alaska, where Mrs. DeGraf stopped on her first trip from Circle City to the Bering Sea, 1895.

was very seasick. When the boat was pitching more than usual one time, she flew right out of the berth, on to the floor, screaming. The captain rushed in to see what had happened, and she implored him,

"Oh, Captain, stop the boat, and let me get off!" Then she would long to be back in Ireland where she could have fresh milk once more before she died, for she had been living on the canned variety so long in Alaska.

She had been a servant in the family of a storekeeper at Forty Mile and married a miner, who afterward struck it rich. She was then going back to Ireland to visit her people. She had with her a lovely skin from a black fox her husband had killed. She said she was going to sell it and take her sister back to Alaska with her. She did sell it to a fur dealer in San Francisco when we landed there, and received $300 for it, which was a good price in those pre-war days.

As the rough weather continued and the passengers showed no signs of recovering from seasickness, the Captain ordered every one on deck. Those who could not, or would not go were rolled up in blankets and carried out. We were a sorry looking bunch of people, spread out on deck, listening to the Captain when he announced,

"I am going to get you people well!"

We could not imagine anything like that happening, and didn't much care whether we got well or not; but he pulled us all through, and the surprising thing was that he gave us each a small glass of Bavarian beer, a few crackers, and a piece of cheese. He saw to it that we swallowed it, and in half a day's time most of us were up and about.

"What became of the rest of the party that came down to Circle City with you", I have been asked. The baker died in Circle, and his wife married again. The Dutchman, who was a tailor by trade, also died there. "Montana" and the Custom Officer went out on the creeks somewhere looking for gold, and I lost track of them.

A friend who had heard my story of this first trip, has remarked that I have given many details about my journey of nearly 5000 miles, and of my sojourn on the Yukon for two years, without mentioning a single mosquito. I can say that the mosquitoes were there. The humpy mounds of damp moss, which are called "nigger heads" up north, appeared to be vast breeding grounds for mosquitoes. These little demons were on hand much of the time and made us quite uncomfortable. We had not provided ourselves with mosquito nets or any other special protection, and were completely at their mercy at times. But we seemed to get used to them; at least the memory of them is not so vivid to me as of the marvelous beauty of the country, the grandeur of the mountains, the majesty of that fascinating, mighty Yukon, and the joy of living in the great out-of doors.

As I recall it now, one or two mosquitoes could give more trouble in Circle City than a whole "flock" of them on the trail. For, after smudging outside and inside my cabin, shutting down the windows tight, and feeling sure I had driven out every mosquito, my rest at night would be disturbed by the singing, and more deadly work, of some of those unwelcome visitors. They bothered the horses and dogs a great deal, and those poor animals suffered terribly from the mosquitoes.

But my long journey at last came to an end. I was back in San Francisco, happy to see my daughter, who had moved from Seattle; but there was no word from the boy. The day after my arrival I took my gold dust to the Mint, and a little later received about $1200 in twenty dollar gold pieces in exchange. It was what I had saved during two years of hard work. When I went to the Mint I was dumbfounded to see the pokes of gold dust piled up on the counter. It represented the clean-ups of those forty miners who had come down on the boat with me. Some of them had as high as $70,000 apiece. They got gold coin for it and put most of it in the bank, spent a small amount having a good time, and then back the next spring for more. I too put my money in the bank, but had to check the most of it out, a little at a time. I rented a rooming house, bought the furniture it contained and thought I would make my home in San Francisco.

2. 'I must have shelter, my feet are freezing'

2

I WAS VERY RESTLESS AND DISSATISFIED in San Francisco. The North had cast its spell on me. Now that I had seen my daughter, I was ready to go back. I thought maybe the boy was up there somewhere in that vast wilderness, and I must try to find him. Then the excitement about the Klondike and Dawson came. I disposed of my rooming house, bought another sewing machine and many bolts of cloth and dressmaker's findings, and once more started for the Northland. But this time my destination was to be Dawson, on the Yukon River, in the Yukon Territory.

The strike on the Klondike fired my brain, and I joined the stampede—not for the gold in the ground, but because I wanted my son, and I knew that I must earn my way on my travels.

On the steamer from Seattle to Skagway, the New York Vanderbilts were passengers. They heard that I had been in the interior and were anxious to talk with me. One of their party hunted me out and asked me, "Are you the lady that used to be in the Yukon?"

"Yes," I replied, "And I am going back again."

"Will you come and have dinner with us?" he asked.

"Who is 'us'?" I want to know.

"The Vanderbilts of New York."

"What do you wish to know?"

"We want you to tell us something about that country."

The man led me into the dining room, to a private table, where there was a special party. The table was set with silver and cut glass and looked beautiful. The captain had on a new uniform, and the ladies were wonderfully dressed. There were seven or eight in their party and they were all very nice to me. I was introduced all around and sat down to a fine dinner with the far-famed family of wealth. I told them some of my experiences on the trail and in Circle City. They plied me with questions and seemed tremendously interested in hearing about that country. They laughed at everything and seemed to have a very enjoyable time, and all thanked me after dinner when I felt that I should go on deck again. But that was about all they knew about that Northland, for they did not get in to Dawson. There were no railroads running into the Interior then, and they had no liking for the hardships of such a long and hard journey over the pass on foot.

There were a number of steamers running then between Seattle and Skagway and they were loaded almost to sinking with freight, and people wild to get in to Dawson and make a fortune. One boat had been wrecked and so there was a shortage. As a consequence, when I was dumped out on the rocks at Skagway, amidst twenty thousand gold-seekers, I waited in vain for my provisions and bedding, then found that our supplies had been left on the wharf in Seattle. Here I was, unable to go forward, and without bed or board, for Skagway could not feed nor lodge this vast throng; each one had to look out for himself.

Being a woman alone, several tried to help me. The captain of the boat on which I had come up from Seattle heard of my plight and sent for me. He told me I could remain on board while the steamer was at the dock. I was very glad to do this. On the vessel was a fine looking, gray haired gentlemen who heard my story from the captain, and spoke to me.

"Lady, you seem to have had a misfortune."

"Yes", I replied, "I am anxious to get on my way to Dawson, but my provisions have not come up."

"Are you looking for gold?" he inquired kindly.

"No, I am seeking my son, and I am going to establish myself in business at Dawson if I can."

"Well, if you are going where gold is, you might as well have some of it if you can get it. I know where there is gold."

"Where?" I inquired eagerly.

"Near the headwaters of the Stewart River," he replied.

He went into his cabin and brought out a map several yards long—a United States Government map—and pointed out three lakes. From one of these, he explained, there runs a river. At the bend of the river there are fortunes in pure gold.

"It sounds like a fairy tale," I said. "If it is there, why don't you go and get it?"

"I have enough of worldly goods," he replied, and with that he took out his card and handed it to me. He was a government surveyor. He had six men with him.

"When you come to Fort Selkirk, below the Five Fingers," he continued, "there is a trail you can see very plainly with the naked eye. Go right across diagonally to the headwaters of the Stewart River to the lakes. Follow down the river to the bend. I would not deceive you. It is there. Only someone who seeks it must go in winter when the ground is frozen. Supplies must be carried in to last a year at a time."

When I came to the place later on, I looked for the trail and saw it plainly from our boat on the Yukon, and I believed the surveyor. I told the story to several young men, but no one would listen to me. They had all started for Dawson; they were going there, and no place else. I believe that to this day no one has found that gold. Right diagonally from Five Fingers I could see the trail, where the animals came down to the Yukon to drink; the trail is so plain it looks as though it had been cut out. But there is marsh land in there, and only after the ground is frozen, could the trip be made. I would enjoy the adventure of trying to find that gold, even at this date, when I am eighty-six years of age.

At Skagway I stayed three days on the steamer, then it pulled out for Seattle and I was thrown on my own resources again for food and shelter. Luckily, I ran across a woman whom I had known in Juneau. She was running a small lunch counter in Skagway and had several tents. I asked her for work to pay for my board and lodging and she needed me. I went to work right away and shared her sleeping tent at night.

While these thousands of people were camped at Skagway, "Soapy" Smith and his gang of robbers turned themselves loose upon the camp. They terrorized the people, and I had my experience too.

One night after my work was done, I went to the tent and lighted a candle and was getting ready for bed. I stooped to unlace my shoes and saw a hand creep underneath the tent. I was terribly frightened at first and wondered if it were "Soapy" himself. But I soon recovered my breath, and I jumped on that hand with both feet, at the same time blowing out the candle so he could not see to shoot me, if he wanted to. In spite of my efforts to hold the hand under my feet, while I called for help, the man got away. I ran to my employer and asked her if she had any money in the tent. She had most of her week's earnings there, and I stayed at the counter while she ran to get it and hide it on her person.

"Soapy" Smith was a gentleman gambler, and had his

trusties who worked for him. He ran everything; he robbed everybody. He had the camp by the throat, until one night there was a mass meeting, and "Soapy" Smith was shot and killed. He lies buried on the hillside in Skagway.

I was compelled to remain in Skagway for two weeks, until my provisions came up from Seattle; and it was a scene of wild disorder, many of the stampeders being delayed as I was, on account of their supplies being left on the dock at Seattle.

At last I was ready to start for the Interior. I hired some white boys who wanted to go to Dawson, to pack my goods. One of them, Johnnie, I had known in Seattle. He had a little mule. The other boys carried everything on their backs, but Johnnie had his mule work for him, until the trail became too steep. Johnnie also had a trombone, and the music he played on it cheered us on our way.

The first time I went over this trail, in 1894, there were few travelers. Now there were so many that in places they

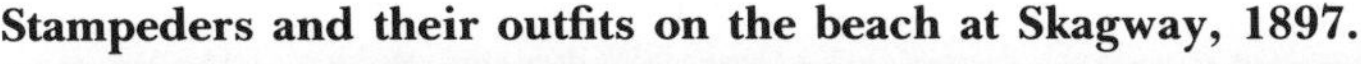

Stampeders and their outfits on the beach at Skagway, 1897.

almost crowded each other off the trail. We had to walk goose-fashion, one behind the other in single file. As far as one could see ahead, and as far as one could see back, down the trail, was that wavering, moving black line of human beings, loaded like pack horses, struggling forward into an unknown country, many of them to perish of cold or starvation. There were thousands of people—all nationalities, and classes. Bankers, clerks, dance-hall girls, gamblers, plumbers, preachers, business and professional men—some with their wives—young boys and men past middle life—all eager to find gold, and grateful for warmth, pleasure, and good cheer along the way.

Just any place they wanted to, when the humor struck them, a crowd would put up a dance hall beside the trail; a large camp would cluster around; whiskey would flow freely; and there would be a carnival of gambling and other dissipation.

At Sheep Camp, a day's travel from Dyea, some boys wearing patent leather shoes and otherwise "dressed up" came and asked me if I would hire them to pack. They were young chaps who had come to the country without preparation for a rough, hard trip. They were discouraged already, their money was slipping away, and the trip was hardly begun. They had provisions, but were trying to work their way into the interior and save their food for future use. I knew the hardships they would encounter, and felt that these patent-leather boys could never make it. I told them, "My sons, you should go home to your mothers. I will buy your provisions, and that will give you passage money home."

It did not take them long to accept my offer. They were relieved to get out of their trouble and go back home. Their idea had been just to have a good time in a wild country, but they found it was a strong man's country, and that gold seeking was, after all, the hardest kind of real work.

Yukoners at Sheep Camp, Dyea Trail, 1897.

A man came to me one morning while I was frying potatoes and onions, as we camped along the trail. He sniffed the air; he was very hungry. I asked him what he wanted.

"I heard you wanted somebody to pack," he said.

"I do," I replied, "but I want a man who is going to stay with the job and see me through to Dawson."

"I won't back out; I am anxious to get to Dawson myself."

He looked at the frying pan and sniffed again. I told him to come into the tent and eat. When he was filled up, I said,

"Come along and help the boys, now."

He started out very well, but each day his courage grew weaker; finally he came to me one morning and said,

"Missus, I guess I will not go to Dawson; I want to go home to my wife, and my feather bed."

He was a big, strong German, and as I looked at him I

had to laugh. When he stopped packing, the boys wanted to know why, and I said, "He wants to go home to his wife, and his feather bed."

All the campers near us heard about it and made life miserable for him, so he did not waste much time starting back to his wife, and his feather bed.

Many men who started out full of courage, weakened and lost their grit early in the journey, and turned back; and it was a good thing they did, for they never could have endured the hardships farther along the way. It takes the trail to find out what kind of stuff is in a person. Men so far from home found temptations on every hand. Fortunes found, or grub stakes brought in from the States, sometimes went in a night at the gambling table.

I had 3000 pounds of provisions, and three boys packing them. The most a strong man would take for a load was 100 pounds, as the way was so rough and uphill most of the time. I camped in Dyea for about six weeks while my provisions were being carried forward to a camp a day's journey ahead. Every morning, as on my former trip, the boys would get up early and I would have breakfast for them at five o'clock. I usually had bacon, beans, evaporated potatoes and onions. I made pancakes, and during the day while the boys were packing, I had time to make bread. Of course, we had coffee. I had to feed the boys well to keep them on the job. Sometimes we had ham, as a treat, and other times the boys would go hunting and we would have moose steak, or mountain sheep.

My boys would pack as far as they could and leave their pack and come back to the tents where I was for supper. A number of boys would go together and pack to the same place and establish a camp together. This way we got to know a good many people along the trail. We were not afraid to leave our provisions alone, for the thief was handled roughly; anyone caught stealing might just as well make his will, if he had any worldly goods to leave.

When I had baked a number of loaves of bread, I would set them out to cool, and men coming along the trail could smell the bread a long way off. They were as hungry as wolves most of the time, and when they would get a whiff of my hot bread they would say,

"That looks good—that bread!"

These men seemed like overgrown boys to me, and my mother heart was touched. I thought of my own son and hoped that, wherever he was, some one would be kind to him. When I had enough bread for my packers and to spare, I would usually give a loaf to some one who stopped to speak about it. I remember one man came up just as I had put out some hot loaves, to cool, and he said,

"Won't you let me have a loaf of it? I will pay you well for it."

"Yes," I said, "you can have a loaf, but I don't want any pay. I will make you a cup of coffee too, if you want it. I have supper ready and waiting for the boys to come home, they will be here pretty soon."

He was so tired and so hungry that he could hardly talk.

"You look as though you had carried a pretty heavy load," I remarked as he sat down.

"Yes, and I am pretty near sick and tired of it. I don't believe I'll go much farther. But you have some nice bread!"

He ate so heartily of the bread, beans, and coffee, that it did my soul good to watch him. When he was ready to go on, I gave him a loaf to take along. He seemed very much cheered up. I did not see that man again until twenty years later. I met him in Skagway, and this is what happened:

"It's Shaw—don't you remember me?" he asked as he held out his hand to me.

"I remember your face. Yes, you're the man who liked my bread, on the trail."

"My, I have never forgotten that feed! I am married now and live here in Skagway. I want you to come home with me and have dinner and meet my wife."

I went, and when he introduced me to Mrs. Shaw, he told her I was the woman who had kept him from starving on the trail to Dawson. He had become manager of the White Pass Railroad, and had a lovely home and charming wife. We had such a dinner as we never dreamed of in the early days in the Northland!

But to get back on the trail.

After the boys had eaten their supper, I had to look after their feet, and moccasins. Many a good blanket I have torn and bound around their feet, after bathing them in hot water and applying some salve I had brought along. Sometimes their feet were so cut and bleeding that it made me heartsick, and their moccasins were torn to shreds on the sharp rocks; their shoes had been worn out long before. I would bind their feet in strips of blanket and wrap them in gunny-sacks, for a few days, until I could make other moccasins for them. It was a hard life, but we had some funny experiences, as well as tragic ones, and a sense of humor helped one immensely.

"What is so funny?" I asked the boys one day when they came into camp shouting with laughter.

"Oh, Mother, if you could have seen what happened!"

"Well, out with it."

"Johnnie was walking along the trail and wanted to take off his moccasins. He sat down on the ground, and in order that the little mule would not run away, Johnnie tied him to one of the legs of his pants. After a while, the mule began to kick, gave a jerk, and a run, and pulled Johnnie's pants off, and there he was!—and you should have seen his face! We had to run after the mule so Johnnie could come back to camp in his clothes."

The little mule could be used to advantage from Dyea to the Scales, but after that he was not able to travel the steep grade, so Johnnie gave his pet to some people who were going back to Dyea, the way we had come. Those who took horses up the trail would have to shoot them at the Scales, or send them back if any one could be found to take them. Months before, horses and mules had been tried for packing on the trail, but the animals with their heavy burdens would topple over the mountain side into the deep canyons beneath, not only losing their own lives, but depriving their owners of the provisions on which life itself depended. So many animals met with accidents here that the canyon below the Scales was called Dead Horse Gulch.

Again, on this second trip, my start on the trail was at Dyea, which was a big settlement by this time—some tents and a few log buildings. It was on the stream that ran down from the mountains. It was called the Dyea River.

At Dyea, Arizona Charlie had a big dance hall and made lots of money. He managed to get it from the boys who came along with packs. It was surely a bedlam camp. The men got drunk, the girls screamed, and the music and racket were horrible.

When I saw it was going to take us some days to pack our stuff from Dyea to the next camp, I made up my mind that we would move farther away from the dance hall and tents, so I picked out a spot on the hillside some little distance away from all the noise and confusion, and finally persuaded the boys to move the tents over there. They didn't want to a bit, but I insisted, and finally we got all settled and were sleeping for the first time in the new location.

About three o'clock in the morning I heard a terrible noise, unlike anything I had ever heard before. I went to the door of my tent and looked out, and then shouted to the boys, but they were so tired and slept so soundly that I could not waken them. I stood there alone looking at a seemingly great black cloud that was rushing toward us. "For God's sake, boys!" I cried, as I ran to their tent, "get up and see what this terrible thing is coming toward us!"

We stood looking down into the canyon where our camp had been. We saw a miner go from his cabin to the creek. He dipped out a bucket of water, probably to get his breakfast, when a great rock fell upon him and cut his head open, and then the great black cloud rushed down and carried everything before it. It swept away the dance halls and most of the tents along the creek, and many of the men and girls who were in its path. A great sheet of water swept through the canyon carrying destruction, while we stood safely on the hillside out of the path of the frightful avalanche. Later we learned that a lake in the mountains had broken its way out and had come rushing down into the canyon with a force and fury that could not be stopped. Many people were killed by falling rocks or trees, and others were drowned.

After it was over, everything was quiet—so very quiet, and the next day the bodies that could be found were buried on the hillside. Arizona Charlie escaped. He and some of his pals were up all night, and they saw the danger in time to save themselves. But he lost everything. In the confusion that followed, some apparently were too frightened to steal, but later tried to lay their hands on other people's belongings. One man was caught in the act. The boys put a big sign on his back that read, "Thief—look out!" and they marched him up and down the camp at the point of a gun until he was worn out, and then they made him leave the camp. We had stayed so long in Dyea, and, although I knew the way was hard and wearisome that lay before me, I was glad to be on my way to Dawson. While we were at the Scales one day, just before the very steep, hard climb, I asked a man who had come back from the summit if he had seen my boys, who had started out early that morning, packing, and he said, "See, away up there." I looked up, and up, and finally did see those boys. They looked like mere specks on the Chilkoot Pass, so high they were.

When we finally got over the summit, it began to rain, and then to snow. The boys went ahead to fix a camp and I followed, slowly, and about four o'clock in the afternoon I found I had to cross a river. I had on high rubber boots and started to ford the stream. The water was bitter cold, and I felt that my feet were freezing. I was frightened, but kept on, and finally reached the other side. I had no idea where I was, but I saw a little way off a small tent in the underbrush. I made for it as fast as I could, and when I was about there a man came out and looked at me.

"Can you let me have a cup of coffee?" I asked, "I want to stop here a few minutes and take off my boots, I am afraid my feet are freezing. Please, let me have shelter for a little while."

"I haven't any coffee," he said gruffly, "and I don't want to take in any travelers; you will have to move on," and turned and went into the tent.

I was in despair. My feet were like pieces of stone; I was hungry and ready to cry, but I braced up and started on, and it was not long before I saw another tent. I managed to reach it, and when I opened it I saw a man lying on a cot, and there were lots of provisions in the tent, but no fire.

"I must have shelter, my feet are freezing, please, may I come in?"

"You bet," said the man on the cot, and he called a big boy and said, "Pull off the lady's boots, and then get a pan of snow, quick!—and put her feet in it." Oh, it was terrible! I saw stars,—my feet pained me so dreadfully. But finally I felt the blood rushing through my feet once more and knew that they were saved.

After a while I felt better, and looking around the tent saw that the man lying on the cot had the most dreadful looking foot I had ever seen.

Going down the Canadian side of the summit from Chilkoot Pass, 1898.

"I shot it," the man explained; "the gun went off accidentally." The foot had not had proper care or treatment and was in an awful condition.

"Whose provisions are these?" I asked him.

"This tent is for shelter for travelers, and the people leave their stuff here when they can't get any farther."

"Well, we must have something to eat, and I am going to cook supper."

"But we haven't any fire," protested the man.

"Well, why don't you have one?"

"The boy says there is no wood around here."

I turned to the boy and said, "Look here, you must skirmish around and get some wood, one way or another. I have money and will pay for it."

The boy was gone about an hour, when he returned with an armload of wood. When he had a fire going, I melted snow and got some hot water and bathed the man's foot. I tore some strips from one of his blankets and bound up the foot, and you can believe he was very grateful!

Among the provisions in the tent I found rice and crackers, prunes, coffee, and some flour out of which I made pancakes. We had a good supper. The boy and man ate greedily as if almost starved, and seemed to gain courage.

This tent was on a hillside. The snow was melting and the water ran down under the tent. There was no place for me to lie down except on a big flat slab-like rock, which was also on a slant, but seemed dry. I found a gunnysack and laid it on the rock, and lay down to get some rest.

As was my custom each night, I thanked God for my deliverance, for food, shelter, and safety, and asked for protection during the night. The man must have thought I was frightened, for he said, "Don't be afraid, Missus, the boys who come in here are a rough lot, but they won't harm you; they are liable to come in any time during the night, but don't be afraid." I told him I wasn't afraid, but that I always said my prayers.

My bed was hard and cold and there was no blanket nor covering of any kind to put over me, but I was so tired that I went to sleep in spite of the cold. I slept so soundly that I never heard a sound during the night. But when I awakened toward morning I felt warm. I sat up on my rock and looked around. There was a candle burning on the crude table in the center of the tent. Around it were seven men, seated on home-made stools, there heads buried in their arms, which were folded on the table. They were all sound asleep—and not one of them had on a coat!! It took me just a moment to discover that they had all taken off their coats and laid them over me to keep me warm.

The men were so kind to me in the morning. They insisted that I lie still and rest until they got breakfast; and they brought mine to me, and it was good. I rested until they were ready to go on their way, and then they took me to the right trail. I found my tent at last, but my boys were not there; they had gone back to the summit for another load.

When I left the men who had shown me my trail, I told them I hoped to see them in Dawson, and one day some months later, as I was walking along the street, I heard a man say, "There's Mother," and another man said, "Yes, sir, that's Mother." I turned around and recognized them, and had them go to dinner with me, and we had a happy reunion.

When my boys got back to camp after packing all day, I always knew they would be hungry as wolves, and one evening when I was busying myself getting supper for them, I heard a man's voice at the tent next to mine, and he asked for a cup of coffee and was refused. I stepped to the opening of my tent and called to him. I asked him if he had seen my boys and he said they probably would not come until morning, that they had been snowed in along the trail. I invited him to come into my tent and gave him hot water to wash with and told him to sit down and eat his supper. How grateful he was—and how he did eat! He gave me his card when he left. He was a San Francisco lawyer. He told me his camp was two miles ahead and that he had a big outfit, and that I was welcome to anything he had. He had been caught in the snowstorm away from camp and was suffering from cold and hunger when he reached my tent. I lost his card, and do not remember his name.

One day we encountered rain, then snow, and more rain, and some of my provisions were not well protected, so my bag of salt melted away to nothing. I asked a man in a little eating house if he could sell me some salt, for I could not make bread without salt, and needed it for other food. He sad he had only enough provisions for himself and was not in the habit of selling any, but I seemed to need it so badly, he would make an exception in my case and sell me a little salt, which he did, charging me $5 for about ten pounds. But I was glad to have it at any price! Farther along I obtained some more salt from a missionary.

We drifted from American into Canadian territory without thinking anything about it, until one day when we were rowing across Windy Arm, I noticed the custom house. I didn't have much money by this time, but I did have a good many provisions, and the question of paying duty suddenly confronted us. I wondered if we had enough money to get us by the Canadian Government officials. The boys could offer no suggestions, and finally I had an idea! I told Johnnie to get out his trombone and play "God Save the Queen!" and the rest of us would stand up in the boat and sing it. I thought it would make those officials feel good; anyway I had read a good deal about Queen Victoria and had always admired her for her good deeds.

So Johnnie played and the rest of us sang as our boat touched the shore. Out came those strapping big fellows, all of one size, and stood still and uncovered while we finished singing. As we landed, they all came down to meet us with smiles and hearty handshakes. They invited us into the house and fed us well. We stayed a day with them, and such a rest and comfort and pleasure it was! I learned later from experience that nothing too good can be said about the Canadian officials in the Yukon. The lives they saved, their kindness to travelers, their courtesy and honor have never been excelled. In Dawson, later when I worked for a fur store, I made many a fur coat for the Canadian Mounted Police, and how proud I was of those coats—and of those men! When I completed one of the outfits, and the officer came in to put it on, the whole establishment would gather around and admire. The coats were fastened with brass buckles, and I can't imagine a nobler figure of a man than one of those boys in his trim, buckled furs. I did not think, when I was at Windy Arm in 1898, as they entertained us, and catered to us, that I should owe my life to them.

Well, when we were ready to go on our journey, the officials shook hands with us and wished us well—and never mentioned a word about duty!

It was getting late in the season. There had been many delays along the way and we still had many miles to go, traveling was hard, the wind was stinging cold, and ice was beginning to run in the Yukon. I felt that we never could get through. I tried to hurry the boys, to push them on so we could make Dawson before the river froze over entirely, but they idled and took every occasion to stop for days at a time until I was almost in despair. My patience came to an end when we reached Lake LeBarge. It was terrible cold and we could find no sheltered place to make camp. I had to sit in the bow of the boat and break the ice ahead, with the paddle, and we progressed very slowly. At last we saw a light in the distance and made for the shore. It proved to be an Indian camp. The Indians saw us coming and came down to meet us. They were glad to see us, for they expected travelers to have money and food, and hoped to get most of it before the boys left. There were a number of young squaws, a lot of whiskey, and the boys went wild. I could do nothing with them. The Indians yelled and howled all night. I found they had stolen some of my flour, and this alarmed me. There was one older man in our party, and I told him my troubles.

"It's a shame the way your boys are acting," he said. So he called them together and told them they must come at

The photographer "gets his man": a Royal Canadian Mounted Policeman is captured in full, formal regalia.

once and help me pack, or he would go with me and they would be left in the camp without food. They laughed and dared me to go without them.

"I will go, just the same," I said, "and the first one that stops me will be shot,"—for I had a revolver with me and would have shot it off, at least to scare them if they had interfered.

They talked together a few minutes and then decided that I meant business. They saw me getting the stuff together, and finally came to help. When we reached the next Canadian police station, I told the officer in charge the trouble I was having with the boys.

"I am going to send a lot of provisions to the boys down on the Hootalinqua", said Major Strickland, "and you can go along with them. My men are packing now. You start on and they will catch up with you on the road tomorrow."

So I started, with my boys, and sure enough the police boys overtook us the next day, and we went together until we came to that dangerous Thirty Mile River. There were six men and the captain, with their two boats, and we were six in number in our boat. They had never been down that river before, but I had, and I knew its rapids and its dangers. I sat in the bow of the second boat and tried to direct them. The water was full of floating ice, and there were big rocks in the bottom of the river, and it was like going through a series of small waterfalls.

We went along for a few hours all right, and the men began to think there was not much danger, and did not heed my directions, as they did at first. But when we came to one of the whirlpools, I saw it, and remembering how our boat had tipped there when I made the trip before, I shouted to them to row to the right. But they thought they were safe and rowed along in the middle of the river.

"For God's sake, keep to the right!" I screamed. The words were hardly out of my mouth before a great cake of ice was hurled at the first boat and the shock threw all the men in the water.

"Now, will you keep to the right?" I asked the men in my boat. They did, and we finally landed on the shore. We threw ropes to the struggling men in the water. One of them got hold of a rope and we pulled him to shore; it was the captain. The others went down, and all the provisions too.

The captain came in our boat and we continued down

the river. It was 60 degrees below zero when we reached the barracks at the Hootelinqua. We stayed there six weeks, hoping from day to day that we could go on. But winter had set in for good. The wolves were driven in by the storm and were so thick that even had the weather cleared, the Canadian officials would not let anyone go any farther. They told me we were welcome to stay at the barracks all winter.

"What! sit here for six months or more with my hands folded! I would go crazy! If you will not let me go on, you cannot keep me from going back. You have lost your provisions in the river; I will sell you mine; and I will go back."

They were glad to get the provisions. They paid me a dollar a pound for the 600 pounds I had left, and added $100 more for the case of coaloil I had, the only one in the country.

It was with a heavy heart that I turned back. The only comfort I had was that it was better than sitting in idleness at the barracks through the long dark winter. The captain of the Mounted Police gave me a letter which I was to present at each station, telling the officers to give me food and shelter, because they had bought my provisions, otherwise they would not have had enough at the Hootalinqua to carry them through the winter.

The stations were about twenty miles apart, and I must reach a station every night if possible. Johnnie and one of the other boys were still with me, the third boy remaining at the Hootalinqua. We had one small sled on which we packed a few needful things, including two small tents to be used in case we could not reach a station at night. Sometimes the boys would pull me on the sled, but I preferred to walk, so as not to make it hard for them. At first I thought I could never stand the long, hard tramp. The wolves were thick and they howled all night long. The days were so short, and we did much of our traveling before day light and after dark at night. Every once in a while we would stop and make fires to scare the wolves away and rest a bit. My limbs ached so from the long walks, but we did our best to get to a station every night. There were always two men at the barracks, which was a big log cabin of one room with a huge stove in the center, and bunks along the walls. The boys would put up my tent outside, and sleep was never more refreshing nor restful than along the trail under those conditions.

After a while I got used to walking and could get along better, but the boys kept getting more weary all the time. One night along about dusk they said they could go no further and sat down in the snow, not caring whether they ever got up or not. But I could not see them give up. I did not want to die of cold or hunger myself, so I urged them on.

"Boys," I said, "It's just a little farther. Around this next bend is Lake Marsh, I know it is! I have been there before, and I remember it well. Just around the bend! Come, get up, and make one more effort to get that far."

But they would not budge; they said they could not go any farther. I hoped I was telling the truth, and I trudged on wearily and prayed constantly, and sure enough, when I got around the bend I saw the lights of Lake Marsh.

Oh, how I called and shouted to them to make them understand. At last they dragged themselves up and stumbled toward me. When they saw the lights, it put new heart into them, and we tramped on until we came to the first cabin, and rapped at the door. It was opened by a man who held a light above his head and peered out into the darkness, and then cried,

"Why, it's the lady who camped beside us at Lake Lindemann"—and sure enough I remembered him. We were hardly inside the cabin before he began to tell us how homesick he and his son were. I spied two bunks, and without ceremony climbed into the top one and said,

"Here I stay until I get rested. Will you have room to keep the boys and me all night?"

They were glad to do it, for they were so lonely.

"We have a Christmas cake," one of them said, "and you shall have supper, with coffee and cake."

After supper I had Johnnie get out his trombone and play "Still is the night, holy the night," and we joined in singing. By and by we heard some one outside the cabin singing, and then some one else, and when we opened the door we found the men from the other tents in that little settlement, drawn together by the music. We left the door open, and we all sang together the different hymns and songs we could think of. I shall never forget that night! All those souls so lonely, and thinking of home and loved ones! Some of them broke down and cried, they were so homesick. But it made them feel better, to sing—and to cry. It was a wonderful, clear night, the stars were so bright and seemed so near, and we sang our hymns in the wilds of the Yukon, for even in that far country we did not forget, "Still is the night, holy the night!"

It was very late when everybody finally went away, and we lay down to sleep. In the morning the whole camp came again. They heard our story, we all sang some more, and when, after we had our Christmas dinner, we started on our way, they walked with us a few miles before they said goodbye.

This delayed us so much, that it would have been late in the night before we could reach the next station so we put up our tents along the side of the trail, and slept cozy and snug. After a week's tramping, in a round-about way, we came again to the custom house on Windy Arm. It was late at night when we reached there. I could hear the dogs barking as we approached. The Canadian police boys had been aroused, and one of them was standing in the door with a lantern when we came up. He held it high, and looked at me, and then slapped his knee and said,

"By Jove, it's the lady who loves our Queen!"—referring to the time, weeks before, on our way down to the Hootalinqua, when we had sung "God save the Queen." He had not forgotten, and he gave us a hearty welcome. It was New Year's Eve.

"You shall have a cabin of your own, tonight," the Lieutenant said, "and tomorrow you shall have turkey for dinner." And so we did, for among their provisions they had a frozen turkey. We laughed and sang and made merry, until a very sad thing occurred. A young man was brought in, with both feet frozen. His legs were just like sticks, they were frozen so hard, and had to be amputated. That cast a gloom over us, for he was a fine young man.

The day after New Year's we felt rested and started again on our way toward home. At Lake Lindemann there was another station of the Canadian Police, and they were always on the lookout for travelers. I was walking along the ice at the edge of the lake, and broke through. The more I tried to get out, the deeper I got in, and was wet and freezing cold. I thought my last day had surely come. I called to my boys who were ahead of me, but they didn't hear my cries; but the Police boys spied me and ran down and pulled me out. Words cannot express my gratitude for being saved!

When we reached Lake LeBarge, I was sitting on a rock eating my lunch, which consisted of hardtack and snow water, when some men passed along the trail, also bound for Skagway. One of them was a photographer, and as he went by he took a snapshot of me with his camera, although I did not know it at the time. Later as I was walking along Second Avenue in Seattle, I saw a picture of myself in a photographer's show window and went in and asked about it. The man then told me of having taken a shot at me when I was eating my lunch that bleak winter's day on the trail. My feet were wrapped in gunny sacks, as shown in the picture, for my shoes had given out long before, from the hard tramp.

My boys and I trudged along, over humpy ice and sometimes on crusted snow which, however, would not bear our weight, and the constant breaking through the crust and getting our feet out again made traveling very slow and tiresome.

When we again reached the summit, there was a heavy snowstorm, and a fierce wind was blowing. The snow flakes were like huge patches of feathers, and came down so thick we were shut in as if by a great white curtain. I exclaimed to the boys, "How will we ever get down from here?" and a man out of the whirl of snowflakes said, "I know that voice, and I will help you down." It proved to be the son of a Judge in Seattle and I knew father and son well. The young man was up there helping some other men lay a cable over the summit. At his direction, we wrapped gunny sacks around us, sat down, joined arms, and started to slide, with him, down the short but very steep winter trail. When we reached the bottom, there were no gunnysacks left! We went with such lightning speed, the sensation was, I imagine, something like being shot out of a cannon.

A little later we were back at Dyea, which was crowded with people, waiting for spring to come so they could go on to Dawson early. The many crude hotels which had sprung up in this frontier town were crowded and I could not find a bed anywhere. The landlady in one hotel very kindly put up a hammock in the kitchen, and I tumbled into it, too weary to take any of the food she urged upon me. The next day we boarded the boat for Seattle, and it was not many days before I was back in San Francisco with my daughter and her family. But still no news of my son!

Anna DeGraf with daughter, son-in-law, and two grandchildren, San Francisco, circa 1900.

3. We got used to 30 and 40 below zero and didn't think much about such weather, but when the thermometer dropped to 60 and 70 below, one could feel it

3

MY FAILURE TO REACH DAWSON MADE ME all the more determined to try it again the following spring. The excitement over the Klondike and Dawson was very great in San Francisco, and I thought the tales of the wonderful strikes might have reached my son and drawn him there. So in the spring of 1899, again I laid in a stock of provisions and some materials, with the idea of starting a little store of my own in Dawson. There were more women in the Northland by this time, and I took along the things I thought they would need. I bought another sewing machine, and started once more for that wonderland.

This time I was successful in reaching Dawson. I rented a little cabin next to one of the hotels which had sprung up like mushrooms in that new rich camp, got my provisions and stock of goods inside, and part of one night's rest, when I was awakened by the crackling of fire, and a great commotion outside my window. The hotel was aflame, and I saw the fire leap to my cabin. I rushed around and saved my featherbed and a few other belongings. My cabin was soon a complete wreck. Some one had carried an old chair into the street and I sat in it until the fire was out, and then kept on sitting there, for I had no place to go. Among the men walking around, there was one who came up quite close and looked at me intently. He finally said:

"Isn't this Mrs. DeGraf, from Seattle?"

"Yes," I replied, "what is left of me; I have been burned out."

"Well, that is hard luck," he said, and added, "Don't you know Reynolds?" It was a man who used to be in a drygoods store in Seattle, where I dealt.

He told me he had taken the management of the Alaska Commercial Company in Dawson, that he knew I could cut and fit and he could give me a job.

He took me, and another woman who was also burned out, over to the Company store, where we had a good breakfast and spent the rest of the night. As my stock of goods had been burned, I took a position with the Alaska Commercial Company in their fur department. Later in the day, I found a room and so started my life in Dawson, with nothing.

In those early days I was very lonely. It was a new, rough camp, crowded with thousands of people from all walks of life, all eager and frantic to make a fortune as quickly as possible.

I had my share of work in that country. I didn't know what a day's rest was, except on Sunday. Then I got up early and took a walk out to the creeks, in summertime, to see what the miners were doing on their claims, and I always scrutinized faces closely to see if by chance any one whom I passed might be my son. It was always so wonderful—the birds singing, the air so bracing and delightful! Then I would go to church and often was invited out to dinner.

A second time I was burned out while in Dawson—not only did this happen to me, but to many others, because some of the buildings were mere shells and burned almost like paper. In the winter everything was frozen up tight, and the only water to be had for fighting fire was from holes cut through the ice on the Yukon, and once a fire started and the wind took a hand, great damage was done and suffering followed. This second fire was caused by a woman hanging some clothes too near a hot stove.

After I had worked for the company store for a few months, people began to come to me to do work for them, so I would work all day at the store and go home and have a bite of supper and sew late into the night for my customers, many of whom were the dance hall girls, and early in the morning I would go and fit the dresses on the dance hall girls, after they had come home from their all-night work at the dance hall. This work was very hard on me, especially during the winter on account of the short days and the extreme cold. We got used to 30 and 40 below zero and didn't think much about such weather, but when the thermometer dropped to 60 and 70 below, one would feel it, although it was a still, clear cold, without wind. It was necessary then to keep a big fire going night and day, and one had to be well bundled up on going outdoors.

In summer, I didn't mind the night work very much, for I could see to sew without a lamp, until midnight. There I would sit by the window and sew, and sew, and friends going by would call to me, "Don't you ever go to bed?"

One night as I was sewing late, the rector of the little English Church came along from a visit to some sick person, and stood in my door and asked if I was ever going to quit work. I said that I would pretty soon. He then said, "Well, put up your work right now, and come home with me and have a little supper." I protested that I was not dressed for visiting, but he insisted that I put on my hat and go along with him. On our arrival at the rectory, his charming wife soon had a lunch for us and we all had a lovely visit.

I went through fire and water and hardships that seem almost unbelievable as I look back on those years—and here I am living yet, and would like to go back to that wonderful country. A judge whom I knew in Dawson used to say many times, "How did you ever live through all those experiences—on the trail, in Circle, and here in Dawson?"—in a country that tries men's very souls and tests their courage almost to the breaking point! But I had a good time, in a way, in spite of the fact that at the bottom of my heart was the constant sorrow of having lost my son. My mother used to say, "You must howl with the wolves, when you are with the wolves," and so I made the best of things up there. Many times my heart did bump—I was so frightened—but I pretended I was just the bravest thing in the world, and got through all right.

You know people in a country like that—along the trail and in the mining camps, in a different way, and better than you could know them in a lifetime in a large city with all its conventions and formalities. Probably I made many a boy and girl think of the mother they had left behind, and I was drawn to them and wanted to help them. Little they knew of the hardships and temptations they had come to; they were inexperienced, many of them weak and inclined to follow the line of least resistance, and were seeking a good time and fortune. A word to some of these steadied them. I was "Mother" all along that trail, and to many in Circle and Dawson. On the trail the boys would say when anything went wrong, "Well, Mother will fix it." Many people knew me by no other name than "Mother." In Dawson, I was called "the Samaritan," because I did what I could to help the dance hall girls and others who needed a mother's advice and counsel.

My needle brought me in contact with all sorts of people, who had many good qualities mixed up with the bad.

Hundreds of dance hall and variety show girls came in to Dawson, some for adventure, others without any idea of the temptations and hardships of that raw, frontier life. There were among them some of the most beautiful girls

I have ever seen—girls in their teens, very attractive, and pleasing in their ways. In working for them, I got well acquainted with many of them and pitied and liked a number of them, for they had some good qualities mixed up with the bad.

One girl, who was exceptionally handsome and quiet in manner, had marvelous talent as a pianist. She did not go on to the dance-hall floor and solicit sale of champagne —which was sold for $35 a bottle, with a $5 commission to the girl selling it. She entertained in one of the rooms off the dance hall, with a musical program. Here she would also serve wine, and the attendant who brought it from the bar was an Austrian count, and was wildly in love with the girl. Often when I would go to try on a dress for her,

The end of the road, summer, 1899: Lake Bennett at the completion of White Pass and Yukon Railway to that point.

he would open the door, and, throwing up his hands, would rave: "Ze Ger-trude, is ze bea-u-ti-ful girl! How I love Ger-trude!" I would say, "Never mind, she is not for you. Go and tell her I want to see her." There were other counts, and barons, and lords aplenty in that country—tending bar and the like.

Early in the morning the town was usually very quiet—those who had spent the night at the dance-halls or saloons having gone to bed. One morning when I had an early errand to the store, on my return I noticed something sticking out of the ditch which ran along the edge of the sidewalk. It was a big, deep ditch, with water in it. On coming closer I saw a girl lying in the ditch—one of the dance-hall girls for whom I did sewing.

It seems she had gotten very drunk and in wandering home in the early morning fell into this ditch. I got a big stick and fished her out, and took her to my cabin, put clean clothes on her, gave her something to eat, and put her to bed. When she had sobered up I talked to her. She was a beautiful young girl, with a wonderful voice. I said, "What do you mean, a girl with your voice and as handsome as you are, getting drunk and throwing yourself away like this!" She cried, "Oh, how can I help it, they all want to have me drink with them. I do not mean to get drunk, but before I know it I have too much." I told her she would have to stop, and asked her what her religion was. She said she was a Catholic. I said,

"All right, you must go this morning with me to the Catholic Church and see the priest, and take the pledge there that you will never touch another drop of liquor." Well, I had quite a time to get her up there.

I asked for the priest, and some of the Sisters came out—they all knew me, and they stood around and looked at the girl curiously. I said, "Yes, I want to see the Father." He came out and I told him what had taken place, and he said, "Why don't you take her to your church?"

I said, "I am not a Catholic, and she is, Father; and would you want me to take one of your congregation to my church?" He said, "Pardon me, I was wrong." So he took her into the church and had her take the pledge that she would never touch another drop of liquor, and I promised him that I would see that she went back to her home in the States. I had my eye on her the rest of the winter and she kept straight. She went out on one of the first boats the following spring.

A few years later as I was walking along the street in Seattle, some one ran up and grabbed me and seemed so pleased to see me. It was this girl. She told me she was married and asked me to come up to her home. I went, and we had a fine dinner and beautiful visit. Her mother was there and was grateful for what I had done for the girl. I did not see the husband, but the girl was loud in her praises of him, and thanked me for having a good husband and good home.

Another time there was to be a masquerade at one of the dance halls, and I was to make the dresses for two of the girls. They were beautiful girls, one a decided blond with lovely curly hair, the other a perfect brunette. They were to be dressed alike, in blue, and the blond was particular that I should make their dresses just right and not disappoint them. That night when I went to try on their dresses, I went up the back way and there was a man standing out in front. There seemed to be an air of something having happened. I saw the brunette and asked her where her little friend was and she began to cry and told me that she was dead. She took me into the room where her chum lay, so beautiful and fair—but now cold and still, when she had been so lively and happy. While we were looking at her, this man came in and stood and gazed at her without noticing anybody else. He then turned on his heel, lit a cigarette and walked out of the room. I thought to myself, "Oh, what men." It seems that the little blond had been very much in love with him, and apparently he with her, and that he always took her to breakfast after the dance hall closed, but that morning he had taken another girl to breakfast, and this made the little blond so jealous and unhappy that she took her own life. The other girls made up a purse and paid the funeral expenses. Another girl took her place, wore her costume that night at the ball—life went on the same, and nobody bothered about her.

On another occasion, I had a dress to make for one of the girls, who was to have a special song in the show, and she cautioned me not to disappoint her. On going to her room the evening of the show, a faint voice called to me to come in. It was time for her to get ready for her turn and I was surprised to find her in bed, and suffering. I got some hot water and helped to make her as comfortable as I could, and asked her what the trouble was. She showed me on her chest the prints like a horseshoe, made by a man's heavy boot—the nail prints of the shoe showed plainly, where he had kicked her; and there was another large wound on the side. She told me that he had come to her door and failing to gain admittance had kicked down the door and acted like a wild man—drunk, of course!

I found out where her home was and urged her to go there as soon as she could travel, that Dawson was no place for her. I arranged with a friend, who was a matron at the Government barracks, to come and nurse her, got a doctor for her, and they did all they could for her. When spring came, she went out on the first boat, and six months afterward word came back that she had died—of the injury received in Dawson. She was as handsome as a picture—a stately brunette, with a voice like a nightingale.

The first winter I was in Dawson I became acquainted with a widow who kept a little store. She was refined and agreeable and we soon became good friends. She was engaged to an engineer and they were to be married in the spring. She brought him to see me and he told us he had some friends who were reading together, studying theosophy, and said he would like to bring them to see us. One was a librarian, another a miner, and the third was manager of the Standard Oil Company there. They were all educated, interesting men. They came the next Sunday evening, and we continued to have these little Sunday evening meetings during the winter. One week we met at the widow's house, and the next at my cabin. The men would read a while, then a discussion followed, and afterward we had a cup of tea and some cake or other light refreshment, and at ten o'clock they all went home. Those evenings were delightful.

As Christmas drew near I suggested to the widow that we ought to do something to keep these men from getting homesick—not anything expensive, but just in a nice way, and she agreed. The librarian and the miner lived in a cabin a short distance out of town on the bank of the Klondike River, and the other men had expected to go out there on Christmas eve. We had to take the miner into our confidence, so we could get into the cabin, and he got the Christmas tree for us.

The afternoon of December 24th the widow and I closed our stores early and the miner came for us with a sled. We had gotten together some little gifts, and toys such as one would buy for small boys—a drum, a watch, a little horn, and so on; and I took along a pair of clean curtains and put them up in place of the ones that had done service for many months. We put strings across the room near the ceiling and hung greens and toys on them; set up the Christmas tree, trimmed and lighted it, had a fire going and supper on the way, when we heard the other men coming. We hid behind the door and waited. One of them said, "Why, Collard (the miner) must have come home early, the fire is going." On opening the door, they exclaimed "Oh, what a transformation! My land! this is wonderful!" Someone inquired, "Who do you suppose did this?" and the Standard Oil Manager, Mr. Tenant, said, "Oh, Mother did it—nobody else!" Then the widow tittered and they discovered us. We danced around and laughed from sheer delight. The miner lay on the floor, kicking his heels together, and tooting on a little horn, as his way of showing his joy. We put big aprons on the men and they finished getting supper, while we set the table.

Afterward we sang hymns and all the other songs we could think of. One of the men read from Shakespeare, and the others took their turns at "speaking pieces." We danced, and as we had no musical instrument except the little tin horn, we danced to our own singing. Either the singing was good or we made a lot of noise that attracted the men from the neighboring cabins and tents, and on looking out we discovered quite a crowd, and they joined in the singing.

When one o'clock came, the men took the widow and me home on the sled—a wonderful ride in the bright, clear moonlight, although the weather was very cold. They had us promise to come again on New Year's Eve, and we went and had another happy time. A sled in that country does not mean the little ones the children have in the States, but it is a large, long, slender Yukon sled, drawn by prancing malamutes or huskies, or sometimes by men.

The people who live in large cities and are surfeited during the Holidays with a round of gaiety, who receive and give loads of handsome presents, wear beautiful clothes and eat all sorts of delicacies, haven't the faintest idea of the wholesome pleasure we had on those two occasions, and at other times, in a simple way. Years afterward, Mr. Tenant wrote me from some place in the States, "Mother, will you ever forget that happy Christmas Eve on the Klondike?"

Anna DeGraf with a dogsled, 24 December 1899, celebrates Christmas in Dawson.

Several married women in Dawson came to me at different times to find out if their husbands went to the dance halls, but, of course, I could not tell them. I did not go to the dance halls, and my associations with the girls was purely on business connected with sewing for them. It certainly would not have been kind to make any wife unhappy by telling her tales about her husband, if I had known any.

About midnight one time a married woman rushed into my cabin; I was still sewing. She said she was worried to death, her husband had not been home for a whole week and I must help her find him, and that if I refused, she would go and find him herself, and with that she pulled out a revolver and showed it to me. She was almost crazy with anxiety, jealousy and sorrow. I knew that one of the dance hall girls had been flirting with him, and I made an excuse to go and try on a dress I was making for her, and see if he was there. When I rapped on her door, I heard a low consultation inside and she said, "Who's there?" I said, "The dressmaker, to try on your dress." I heard her say, "Oh, she won't say anything" and she opened the door. Sure enough, there stood that man. I said to her, "I have your dress to try on", and she took it into the other room. This gave me a chance to whisper to him that he should wait for me downstairs, that I had something to tell him. So I fitted the dress, and when I went downstairs, he was waiting for me.

I said, "Look here, you must go home." He said, "What have you got to do with it?" I said, "I have got a great deal to do with it. If you want to know it, your wife is over in my shop with a revolver, and if you don't go home you will be a dead man tomorrow; she means business and that is all there is to it." And I roasted him good. He promised me he would go home, and he did, for I made it my business to find out if he kept his word. But he didn't learn a lesson. He followed this girl to Fairbanks, and his wife went back to the States. When his money was gone, the girl cast him off, and he came sneaking back to Dawson and appeared at my door one day when I was just having dinner.

"Where is my wife?" he demanded.

"Why should you be looking for a wife? Did you think she would be waiting patiently here for you, ready to forgive you again?"

"I know it," he said, "I am not worthy that she should take me back," and he went on upbraiding himself. He became very humble and broke down, and then he had some dinner. He said, "Do you know that not another person in Dawson has offered me as much as a glass of water? I have suffered terribly in body and mind, and I want you to write a letter to my wife and tell her how sorry I am, and ask if she won't take me back. She won't listen to me."

"All right, when I get time I will," I said.

"No," he urged, "do it right now and I will mail the letter."

And I did write the letter for him then and there and he hurried to the post office with it. After many weeks, an answer came that she would forgive him, and he went back to the States on the next boat. They wrote me that things had been fixed up between them. I saw them in their home later when I went outside and they were happy and prosperous.

In another case, I went to the Post Office in Dawson with a man, whose wife I had known in the States, and at my urgent solicitation he had a money order made out in her favor for six hundred dollars. As I went home I was so joyful thinking how much good that money would do the wife and children, and was heartsick when I found out afterward that he slipped back to the post office and had the money order cancelled, and spent that sum of money in wild dissipation.

There was plenty of amusement in Dawson for those thousands of restless, homesick people. One man who now has a chain of vaudeville houses up and down the Pacific Coast and who is know to his friends as "Alec" Pantages, came into Dawson in the early days and conducted a variety show for a number of years in what was called the Opera House. Here he put on fine entertainments for the miners. One summer, a special feature was the dancing and singing of two dozen young, beautiful, and talented girls. He sent to Paris for a French dancing master, who taught the girls the minuet. They wore powdered wigs and costumes of satin and velvet—all of the time of Louis XIV, and half of their number were dressed as young men. I made the costumes and everything had to be of the finest materials obtainable, and correct in every detail for the period represented. There was a complete change of costume once a week, and I made all their suits, and you can imagine I was busy, with that and all my other work. This man, "Alec," was just fine to work for.

He was very just, prompt to pay, and paid well, and was a past master at his business, being able to judge quickly and accurately of an applicant's ability.

Later another theatre or opera house was built and here men would take their women folks. One year Frohman had a stock company in there. Ralph Cummings was the leading man and was a fine actor and a polished gentleman. The leading lady was charming and an actress of ability. I did a great deal of sewing for her, in fact, made the costumes for the different plays put on. Many times I had dinner with her and Mr. Cummings, and I have never been in more delightful or entertaining company.

One day when I went to deliver a dress to her, I was feeling quite ill and on going into the warm room, fainted. She called Mr. Cummings and the two of them took me home after I had regained consciousness. He ran over to the store and got two plasters and put one on my chest and the other on my back. They built a fire for me and wrapped me up warm in blankets, and sent a nurse to look after me and then went to the theatre. After the play was over, about midnight, they came again to see if I was comfortable. The nurse stayed with me, and in four days I was all right again. I then learned that Mr. Cummings had studied medicine, intending to be a physician, but had given this up to go on the stage. The plays of this company were delightful. They gave us the "Charity Call," "The Second Wife," and a lot of good plays. The cheapest seat in the house was $5 and they ran from that up to $25.

After I had been in Dawson for seven years, I came outside to visit my family, get a change of climate, and buy a stock of goods to take back in the spring. The trip was made by boat to Whitehorse, and then by train to Skagway—quite different from the trips I had made over that long, hard trail on foot.

When I left the steamer at Seattle, there were no taxis or cabs at the wharf, so I decided to walk up town to my hotel. I was loaded down with bags and bundles and boxes, and must have looked like an Irish immigrant. As I walked along I was attracted by a vaudeville showhouse which had "Aleck's" name on it, and a sign in front announced that Lucia di Lammermoor was to be sung at the matinee that very day. I dropped my bundles right there

A double-headed freight train on the "Steel Bridge" over Dead Horse Gulch, just south of White Horse Pass, circa 1900.

in front of that sign, and asked a policeman where I could leave them while I went to the show. He suggested that I take them to the box office, so I did, and the young man there kindly took charge of them. I bought my ticket and went into the show. I had not been to the hotel yet, but I didn't care—I was having a good time, and was so hungry for good music. I had a front seat in the first balcony and the show was wonderful! Then I got my bundles together and went to the hotel. I had supper and went to another show that night.

After a good night's sleep I strolled downstairs a little late that next morning, and when I came up to the clerk's desk someone grabbed me by the arm, and said, "For goodness sake, old soul! where did you come from?"—just like that. And, behold, it was my actor friend, Ralph Cummings, whom I had enjoyed knowing and seeing act in Dawson. He said, "Have you seen Aleck?" I said, "No, but I have been to his theatre, and I enjoyed it immensely." He said, "Well, you must go with me and see Aleck." So we went, and we saw Aleck, who told us he was now settled down and married, and urged me to go up to his home and meet the wife; but I was too busy and expected soon to leave for San Francisco. Aleck gave me a box seat for that night's performance; it was "Lord Chumley," and Mr. Cummings was the leading man, and there were others in the company whom I had known in Dawson. They recognized me, and I tell you we had some fun that night! They were constantly putting in remarks that were not in the play, and asking me questions across the footlights into that box, and the audience supposed, of course, that it was all in the play. It was most amusing. Mr. Cummings was surely a fine actor, a gentleman, and I am sorry that I have never seen him since.

4. To one who loves to study human nature, this big, overgrown, raw mining town of Dawson was a source of never ending interest

4

After a few years the government officials, officers of the mining companies, lawyers, and other business men, and the miners even, brought in their wives and children, and I did a great of sewing for them. So I went outside about every two years, after my first long stay in Dawson of seven years, and bought goods for my shop.

On one of these trips there was a little boy who had been a bootblack and had his stand in front of a dance hall called the Opera House. His name was Johnnie. When I saw him on the boat, all dressed up, I said, "Why, Johnnie, what are you doing here?" He grinned and said, "I am going outside to my mother." He came nearer and whispered that he had three thousand dollars. I told him not to let anybody know but to take it to the captain and have him keep it in his safe. I went with him and he turned his gold dust over to the captain. He said his mother lived in Pullman and that the money would help her pay off a mortgage on their home. I went with him to the bank when we arrived in Seattle, and after keeping out a little to pay his railroad fare, he deposited his wealth in the bank and then started for home. He was fourteen years old when he left Dawson, after being in there several years. When he heard the tales about the gold strikes on the Klondike, he determined to go, and he worked his way on the boats to get there. It took courage for a little chap like that to go into that far country and make his own living and save so much. He used to sweep out the dance hall in the morning and there was always a lot of gold dust that had been spilled on the floor and he used to save it and keep it in his cabin where he lived alone. The men around the dance hall knew he did this, and it was with their permission, for they admired his pluck.

On my trips to the States I was always running across some one from the Yukon country, and had interesting experiences. One day in San Francisco I met a girl who had been in the variety show in Dawson and had married a gambler, who had made a big stake on Bonanza Creek. The claim was so rich he could go around and pick up handfuls of nuggets from the top of the ground. He took out a hundred thousand dollars in a short time. He used to carry nuggets around in his coat pockets until they bulged out on the sides in big humps. The day I met her down in San Francisco, she urged me to go over to the Palace Hotel with them, where they were staying. We had a good time talking over the old days in Dawson, but the husband stayed right there, although she tried to invent excuses to get him out of the room. Not being content to sit on a chair, he lay on the floor right by us, like a big dog or Little Lord Fauntleroy. He was so jealous of her that he would scarcely let her out of his sight. As I left the room when my visit was over, she whispered to me to meet her the next noon at a popular restaurant, and I did, and she had been successful in slipping away from him, for she was alone, when she met me. She bombarded me with questions about her old friends in Dawson.

When I was ready to go North again in the Spring, as I could not tell definitely how soon the ice in the Yukon would break up so the boats could run, I often had to wait at Whitehorse from one to four or five weeks, as did others. Sometimes when I wanted to get into Dawson before the spring rush on the first boats, I went very early and took the stage from Whitehorse while the winter trail was still good—the trip from Skagway to Whitehorse being made very comfortably by train.

On one of these trips, the company operating the stage charged me $40 for taking in one ordinary trunk, in addition to the $100 I had paid for my fare from Whitehorse to Dawson. I felt it was an exorbitant price, but had to pay it, and told the agent I would get even with the company sometime, but hadn't any idea how, or when, I could do it. On a later trip, however, when I was going in by stage, I met at Whitehorse a young man called Fritz whom I knew in Dawson, and he told me he was now running an independent stage and said he would charge me only $50 for my fare and take several trunks I had, free of charge. He assured me he had plenty of equipment, so I arranged to go with him. On the way back to my hotel I met five boys who had come up from the States at the same time I did, and told them how I was going to Dawson and they said they would like to go along but had no money to pay their fare, that the regular stage would take them in C.O.D. as they were going to work for the Guggenheims. I took them to Fritz and told him they would surely pay him after they got to Dawson, and he agreed to trust them.

Several more heard about Fritz and his stage, so there were ten of us that went with him. The women who had come up with me and who had their tickets on the regular stage vowed vengeance on me for carrying off all the young men. We had great fun on this trip and it was a race all the way to see which stage would get to a roadhouse first for the night, and Fritz usually came in first at the various stops along the way.

The minerals that are buried in that country—it is hard to believe! If I were a young man, with no one

White Pass and Yukon Railroad locomotive #7 (still extant in Dawson City) on the trestle over Glacier Gorge, at the entrance to the only tunnel on the line (some 250′ long), circa 1900.

dependent on me, I would certainly go back to that Yukon country and prospect, and make myself independently rich. Wherever you go, in that country, there is gold—placer gold, or quartz gold. Those who know, will tell you that the surface has only been scratched.

In Dawson there are all kinds of people and of about every nationality. Most of them seem to know about anything but mining. They knew precious little about that, and most of them were not accustomed to hardships.

I recall one man whom the others delighted to call a "Tenderfoot," because they thought he was so much more ignorant than even the common run of them. There were two men staking out a claim on a hillside and the Tenderfoot wandered up to them and asked if there was any chance of his staking there. They growled at him and said they had no time to bother with a Tenderfoot, for him to go yonder in the hills and look for gold. They laughed as the fellow wandered away. He went up the gulch and after months of absence came back again and found these two men still working their claim.

"Well," they jibed, "where you been? Did you get anything?" He put his hand in his pockets and pulling out some nuggets, said, "Do you call them 'anything'?"

They dropped their tools and grew quite excited and asked him where he got them. He described the place. They went up there with great speed and staked next to him. The young fellow went to the Recorder's Office in Dawson and recorded his claim as "The Tenderfoot." His strike was the first in the gulch, which proved to be a place rich in nuggets.

A man who chopped wood for me in Dawson said one time that he had been up in the copper country where a big mining company was at work. An expert had gone in there from New York to make investigations on the White River. When he reached there, he threw up his hands, and exclaimed, "My land, what wealth." His company secured the property and it was very rich.

Later I knew a man up there who wanted to send out a slab of the copper to the Seattle Fair. There were six horses trying to pull it along the trail, but they could not make it. There was no roadway in that section and this immense slab of copper could not be dragged thru the woods. It had to be left and people going the trail had to climb over it or go round.

In Dawson, mule teams, horses, and dog teams were hauling gold dust in from the mines all during the night, to the Bank of Commerce, which was big log house, with strong vaults. This kept the boys in the bank working late, and it made them cross, for they could not go to the dances like the others could.

I did a little staking of my own. The tip was given me by a woman who cooked for the boys in the bank. She sent for me one day and said she had heard there were rich deposits on Hester Creek. She could not leave the bank to go, but said if I would go she would send a man with me to stake for her, and I could stake next to her claim. I said I would try. She warned me that the police boys were all going out to stake there and that I must get ahead of them.

There were five in our party and we didn't have much of a start on the police boys. We had to walk, and it was bitter cold. After a long tramp we came to a little coffee house and went in to get warm and have a cup of coffee. As we sat at the counter I looked out and saw the police boys coming, five of them. We dropped our cups, slipped out the back door and made a run for it. We took a cut-off and got there first. We had just finished measuring our claims and had our notices posted when the police boys ran up.

"By George," said one of them, "the lady got ahead of us!" The next thing was to get to the Recorder's Office. We hurried back to the coffee house. I went out and talked to the cook to see if he knew of someone who was going to Dawson. He said there was a man in the other room who was, and he had a dog team too. I bargained with the man and he took me flying to the Recorder's

Office and I was the first to register a claim on Hester Creek, which afterward proved to be rich.

Those who staked were required to do a certain amount of work on a claim each year and pay a specified assessment. I put in my first year's work and paid my first assessment, but was outside in the States when the second year came around, and I had so many things on my mind which kept me from getting back or sending back money in the required time, so when I finally did return to Dawson, my claim had been jumped.

A number of times after this I went on trips to stake claims, but on only one other occasion did I succeed in finding a claim that promised well. This was on Nine Mile. It was at night, during extremely cold weather. We had to climb the Dome, a hard and rugged way. We had not gone very far before we were lost. The howling of wolves was terrifying. We had one little sled but none of us could ride in it because the hillside was too steep and rough. We were just wandering around aimlessly in a circle when we stumbled onto a little cabin. It was locked, but we broke into it. We found food, cooked and ate it, and rested until daylight.

Taking a piece of paper which I found in the cabin, I addressed a note to the owner, telling him that we had to break into his cabin because we were lost and freezing; that we had used some of his provisions, and that if he would send a bill to Dawson or come to see me the next time he was in Dawson, I would settle with him for the food and shelter we had in his cabin, and, thanking him, signed my name.

Some weeks later a man called at my cabin and said he was the one to whom I wrote the note, that there was no charge, and that he was glad we had used the cabin. We had a pleasant little visit, but I never saw him afterward.

The next morning after spending the night in the

miner's cabin, we started out again, got over the Dome all right, and down into French Gulch, where we staked. On the way back I could not keep up with the rest of the party and kept falling back farther and farther until they were out of sight. I was cold and discouraged and feared that I might freeze to death. Again in my need I came to a miner's cabin. The miner kindly gave me a cup of coffee and let me stay and get warm. I hoped a dog team might pass so I could ride down to the Hotel Dewey, where our party had planned to spend the night, but none came. I started to walk on, and then ran to keep warm. It got dark and I found I was in a maze of sluice boxes. I felt very lonely and helpless. I went one way and then another, but could not find any way out from among the tangle of sluice boxes. Finally I saw a man not far away turning a windlass. I called to him to come down and help me to find my way out.

"Too damned cold!" he curtly replied, then blew on his hands and started to turn the windlass again, his body silhouetted against the sky by the light of a bonfire near by.

"Tell me where the Dewey Hotel is," I shouted.

"Too damned cold!" he replied a second time.

"Come down and take me to the hotel and I'll give you a dinner, and a drink that will warm you." He couldn't resist that invitation; men in that country are always hungry—and thirsty! Down he came and he led me out of the network of sluice boxes. I never could have found my way out alone. By this time the moon had come up and it was a glorious night and we soon covered the two miles to the hotel. I kept my promise, and then joined the woman and three men who made up our party. What I said to them about deserting me need not be recorded here!

The Hotel Dewey was a big, two-story building of logs, very long, with a hall running through the middle, rooms on both sides. There were, in fact, only two great rooms, one on either side of the hallway, and these were partitioned into sleeping quarters by flimsy curtains, each section with two bunks, one above the other.

After supper, I asked for a room for the other woman and myself. We were given a candle and shown into one of these curtained compartments.

"Now, we shall have a fine sleep tonight!" I said.

We were both too tired even to talk, so went to bed expecting a good night's rest. But it was not long before the miners began to come into the hotel. One of them had enough whiskey to make him feel happy and he began to sing "Rosy O'Grady, my dear little Rose" to the woman who was with him. She tried to stop him and demanded liquor.

"We will get married bye and bye" he sang, at the top of his lungs.

Again she tried to stop him, rang a bell and ordered some champagne, all of which could be distinctly heard all over the place. They drank and talked, howled and sang. Nobody tried to stop them. Finally the man, getting up from his chair, evidently reeled, and fell headlong through our curtain-partition onto the floor just beside my bunk. The crash of his heavy body falling roused the people all over the hotel and they came running in and dragged him back to his room, put him in his bunk, and there was no more noise from that quarter.

But all night long the men came and went in the barroom below. The floor of our room was of the roughest boards and we could look down through the wide cracks and knot holes and see the men shoving their gold dust across the counter and drinking until they could hold no more. We had little sleep that night. The dance hall was right next door and kept up a racket until the early morning. I got up and dressed and stepped outdoors, and what a wonderful sight there was! Gold Hill was right in front of the hotel and it was aflame with many fires leaping toward the sky, like an illumination for some great occasion.

The miners had to build these fires to thaw the ground so they could dig out the pay dirt. They would buildthe fires at night, then next day dig out the thawed ground. After a few weeks of this process, they would rig up a windlass and bring the dirt to the surface. Two men usually worked together, one at the top on the windlass and the other in the mine loading the loose dirt into the bucket, hoist it, and it would be piled up in a dump. In the spring there would be the clean-up, when there was water to wash the gold from these dumps that dotted the country. Some of the nuggets found in that section were as big as hen's eggs, this being one of the richest gold deposits in that country.

When I came down to breakfast the next morning, I said to the proprietor, "What kind of a hotel do you keep here?"

"I knew you wouldn't like it," he said, "but you know we are all here to make money. When the miners come in to have a good time, they spend their gold dust here and at the dance hall, and we want our share."

We learned that we had been followed to French Gulch. When people would find a good claim up there, they usually went to stake it at night. Just because they tried to keep it secret—slipping out of town after dark to stake—every one else would naturally think a rich strike had been found, and would follow, and if enough people knew about it and got excited a stampede would follow. But this didn't bother me. I had measured off my distances, to the north, east, south, and west; had written my name on the claim, and no one could touch it, lawfully, inside of a year.

The stage came about nine o'clock that morning and took us back to Dawson. We soon had our claims recorded. Sometimes there would be so many in line waiting to get their claims recorded that men, and even women, would take their blankets, and food, and camp in front of the Recorder's Office all night in order to be there early the next morning.

Oh, the prices many paid for their gold in that country! Their legs and arms, their reputations, their happiness, comforts, even necessities, and their lives!

A woman and a man started from Dawson to go to Forty Mile. They had heard of some good claims there, and even though it was extremely cold weather, they wanted to stake them. A snowstorm overtook them and they lost their way. Their arms and legs were frozen. They had lain down in the snow to die when they were rescued and brought into Dawson. Their legs had to be amputated, leaving them just stumps for the remainder of their lives—all for a bit of gold! The people in Dawson took up a collection, and the Canadian Government looked after them.

It is not alone the severe weather that took men's lives, but there were robbery and murder in the first few years, although it is remarkable the way the Canadian Mounted Police kept order. In this one instance, a man left Dawson with $60,000 worth of gold dust on his sled. He was going outside to his family. When he reached the Mindo Road House, he stayed there all night. Among the many men who stopped there were two who in some way found out that this traveler had a lot of gold dust with him. They knew the way he would have to travel, for he was making the trip alone instead of on the stage, so they started first and got ahead of him. When they came to a high bank, they stopped and waited for him to come within hailing distance. Then one of them called out, "Partner, come over this way," the river isn't frozen there where you are; you'll fall through the ice."

He turned off and went up the slough where they

were. They fell upon him and killed him, dug a hole in the ice and shoved the body under, and made off with the gold dust. It was not many days before the Mounted Police found the body, and started a search for the murderers. After many months one of them was brought back to Dawson. He was kept in the log jail, tried, and sentenced to be hanged. He planned to escape through the roof. It was discovered what he was doing, and day and night relays of the police boys sat guard on the roof with their guns, in the severe winter weather, and when he finally broke through the roof, he looked down the muzzles of two guns and was told to get back downstairs, which he did speedily. At eight o'clock one morning soon after, he paid the extreme penalty for taking another man's life. The bells tolled while he was being hanged, and it was a most doleful time. The other man was never brought back during the long period I was there, which leads to the belief that he must have died or been killed, for it is claimed that the Mounted Police, when once assigned to a case, never let up until they find their man, whether the search takes them to South Africa or any other part of the globe.

In that country they made a great deal over a hanging, in order that all ruffians might beware of a like fate. Laws were very rigid, and were enforced. For minor offenses there was the woodpile in the Dawson jail yard, where the prisoners had to work outside at 60 below, under guard. They were all afraid of that woodpile!

The loneliness and privations of those gold-seekers were pitiful. Most of them lived in little cabins on the creeks, month after month, unable to cook the proper kind of food, and they became ill. Many of them suffered so much from homesickness that they went wild when they came into Dawson, and even good men did many things then that in other circumstances they would have looked upon with horror. The Mounted Police (without their mounts) patroled the streets of Dawson, so that I felt perfectly safe.

One Christmas Eve in Dawson, as I was on my way to dinner at the hotel, I saw a man and woman with two little girls standing in front of a store window where there was a display of dolls. I learned that this family had been fifteen years in the wilderness; that the children had been born and raised—you could not say "brought up"—in a cabin out in the hills, far from any appearance of civilization. The children had never seen a doll before, had never been to school, nor played with other white children. One must have been twelve, and the other perhaps ten. They stood there with their mouths and eyes wide open, with wonder and delight.

Another miner said he had not seen a white woman

The well-regulated militia of Dawson identifies its members with sashes. Firearms seem not to be part of the daily uniform, though they were available if required.

for ten years—he had been out on his claim, a long way from Dawson.

In the summer time the vegetables grew rapidly, and I have never seen such fine gardens as were had in Dawson by those who could stop hunting gold long enough to spade up a garden. There was an abundance of wild berries, and the country was a-bloom. For one who loves nature, it was worth going through the long, severe winters, just to be alive in the spring and summer in that wonderland.

While the substantial things were plentiful—the staples being brought in from the outside in quantities by the boats, the men longed for pie and cake and other good things they used to have at home. When apples first were brought in, they were a wonderful treat and cost 25 cents apiece. Oranges were 50 cents each. Many a woman made a small fortune by cooking in the Yukon Territory, and across the line in Alaska camps. One of these had a place up on Bonanza Creek called "Mary's Coffee House." When she left Dawson, after seven years, she carried with her fifty thousand dollars, and she had not been mining. She had a big log cabin, where men could eat her pies made of dried apples—but wonderfully good!—and doughnuts with good coffee; or they could take the pies and doughnuts to their cabins to supplement their monotonous menu. She charged $1 apiece for the pies—and her doughnuts were as good as any that ever were made in New England!

Another woman took advantages of the lack of bath tubs in those first days in Dawson. She brought a great tin bath tub over the trail, and set it up in her tent on the edge of the Yukon River, where it would be easy to carry water. She charged $1, or its equivalent in gold dust, for a hot bath, and would also wash the bather's clothes, if desired, charging $1 for a woolen shirt, and so on. Her tub and clothes line had no idle hours! In two years she had coined ten thousand dollars. Later, when barbers came into the country and opened shops, they put in bath tubs; but this woman had the trade all to herself in the first two years.

When miners came to town, they usually had a regular eating jag. They were hungry for everything except evaporated potatoes and beans and bacon. I remember seeing one miner come into a little restaurant in Dawson. He had been out of sugar at his cabin for a long time and was craving it. He grabbed the sugarbowl from the table where he sat and bagan to eat the sugar by the spoonful. The waiter remonstrated and explained that the sugar was for coffee.

"Never you mind about the coffee," the miner said, "I'm going to eat this sugar as long as I want to." He ate it all, and then said, "Now give me some sugar for my coffee." He paid $2.50 for the bowl of sugar, and was glad to get it.

Another time a prospector came into a restaurant where I was and said "Gim-me some of them there fresh eggs! I want a plenty!"

The waiter brought in half a dozen fried eggs, with coffee and bread. The man ate them ravenously, and called, "Gim-me some more eggs!" Again the waiter brought in a half a dozen, and kept this up until the customer had eaten twenty-two eggs. I sat there and counted! He took out a poke of gold dust that must have held several thousand dollars worth, and paid $22 for the eggs—$1 apiece, with the bread and coffee thrown in—and gave the waiter a $5 tip. The so-called "fresh eggs" were at least several months old, having been sent up from Seattle before navigation on the Yukon closed.

After the Yukon froze over and the days grew very short and it was extremely cold, we had a lonesome feeling; but after a while we cheered up and made the best of it. We had to get up entertainments and dances. Ice skating was a favorite sport with many. After the school house had been built, we had a dance on the ice in front of it one night, as a novelty. The men built bonfires all around it in a circle; they gathered together a band, and we danced in the open, then went to a nearby restaurant for refreshments.

We had quite a number of Pioneer Dances. Each white woman usually had more invitations than she could possibly accept. Then there was a reception at the Governor's House when George Black became Governor of the Yukon Territory. He invited everyone in the country; it was open house, and began at three in the afternoon and lasted all night.

As I walked toward the house I noticed in front of me two young miners, hardly more than boys. They had on brand new overalls and new hats. They were so dressed up that I felt sure they were going to the reception. But when they got to the house and saw the crowds, they stopped, and then went on past. The Governor spied them, for he came running out and called after them:

"Here, you fellows, come in; this reception is for you. It doesn't make any difference whether you have on overalls or a swallowtail. You come in and enjoy yourselves."

He took them in and gave them a hearty welcome. People were there in all kinds of clothes, from the handsome gowns sent over from Paris, France, to the wives of the millionaires, to the worn, shabby outfits of those less fortunate. It didn't make any difference to the Governor or his good wife. The house was beautifully decorated, as it was summertime and the flowers were plentiful and lovely. There was a wonderful supper, and then we danced. Mrs. Black introduced me as the oldest pioneer in the Yukon, and appointed two pretty young girls as my attendants for the evening, to see that I did not lack for attention. I shall never forget that night!

To one who loves to study human nature, this big, overgrown, raw mining town of Dawson was a source of never ending interest. My sewing brought me in contact with the most refined, cultured ladies as well as those of the other extreme. I spent many happy hours in the homes of some of the loveliest people I have ever known. The family of a Judge I remember with great pleasure. The wife was a talented musician, as were her two daughters, whom she took to Leipzig while I was in Dawson, where they spent three years finishing their musical education.

One evening I went to a musicale and had a most enjoyable time, for good music is to me like water to a thirsty person. One young man played beautifully on the violin, and on leaving I told him how delighted I had been with his music, and what a treat it had been. Not long after that he appeared at my door one evening, very much dressed up. I invited him in, and asked him to excuse me for continuing to sew, for I had some work I must finish. He seemed ill at ease, and after floundering around a good deal, said he had come to ask me to marry him. I was astonished, and doubtless showed it. I assured him I was too busy making a living to take unto myself a husband, and I made it so clear to him that I could not think of having such a luxury as a husband, that he did not tarry long, and the subject was never mentioned to me by him again.

The widow whom I met when I first went to Dawson, married the engineer the second winter, and I and a man some years younger than myself, stood up with them, at the Presbyterian Church, where no one else was present except the officiating clergyman. Just before the ceremony was to be performed, the best man looked around, cleared his throat and said, "Well, Mrs. DeGraf, if you are willing, we might as well make this a double wedding." But again I was forced to seem heartless, for I objected most positively and there was only one couple married on that occasion.

A capitalist who was heavily interested in mining property around Dawson, had his family come on from New York one summer for the trip. The women were privileged to go anywhere, and laughed at what they saw. They seemed to think we were strange creatures unlike other people in the world.

I had met them, and so they paid me a visit one day. They were not at all bashful about making remarks about my cabin, which had been furnished by my landlady, and was comfortable. At any rate it was my home; I lived there and had my little store in it. The furniture was all hand-made by some of the men around the camp, and very crude. The bed was of rough lumber, with cretonne stretched over it to make it smooth. I had my feather bed, which I had brought from Germany as a girl, and had carried back and forth to the States on my various trips. I had some blankets and a big bearskin to keep me warm.

"Oh, here is a home-made bed!" exclaimed one of them. "Let's sit on it and then when we get back to New York we can tell the friends that we sat on a home-made bed in a woman's cabin in Dawson!"

They looked around the cabin, examining things critically and laughing at what they found, and continued to remind each other how much fun it would be to tell about all this when they got back to New York.

This was not an isolated case, either here or in other parts of the far North. I was told of instances where tourists, on leaving the boat at Juneau, would stroll around the town, open the doors of houses, without knocking, peer inside and comment about what they saw, and exclaim at seeing curtains at the windows.

It is claimed that the mining towns of Alaska and the Yukon Territory have a greater number of college graduates, both men and women, in proportion to the population, than any other settlements. This is due largely to the fact that scientific men are drawn there to work for the mining companies, or independently—and lawyers and doctors are also to be found there.

I was told of one case where a highly educated man was traveling through the North on a lecturing tour. He too happened to be from New York City. An accident happened to the vehicle in which he and some other men, whom he had never met before, were riding, One of the men in the party who was dressed as a frontiersman, jumped out and began to tug and pull to get the wheels out of the ruts and helped to make repairs. As they continued on the trip, the New Yorker became interested in the frontiersman, and began to engage him in conversation. He sympathized with the frontiersman because he lived in such a God-forsaken country, where there were no creature comforts nor cultured people. He was chagrined to find out, at the end of the journey that his companion was a Harvard professor, who went North every summer for his vacation, and worked for a mining company in the laboratory; and that his wife went with him, and they looked on it as a great adventure and pleasure trip, and at that time his wife had visiting her two Vassar graduates, schoolmates. He told the New Yorker that at the mines they lived in a modern house, lighted by electricity and heated by steam.

5. The arrival of a great grand-daughter caused me to say good-bye to the Northland

5

WHEN THE ICE BEGAN TO BREAK UP and run out of the Yukon River in the spring, there was much excitement and great rejoicing. Everyone was so happy that the boats would soon be running down from Whitehorse. It was great sport among the men to bet on the exact time when the first ice would break, and lots of gold dust and nuggets changed hands at that time.

It is a wonderful sight—that breaking up of the ice. The warmth of the sun melts the ice, and it breaks off in huge pieces, some of them of tremendous size. They rush down all the side streams and join the mass of crushing, crashing cakes of ice in the main stream, and pile high. They crown the mighty Yukon so that big pieces are pushed up on the banks and sweep the shores clean for miles. On and on this mass of ice goes, down to Bering Sea—a tour of over 2000 miles! Although the breaking up of the ice takes place in June, it is not until July that the boats come up the river from St. Michael, and sometimes the ice is not all cleared out of the river before freezing sets in again. I have known summers when no government boats could come up the river from St. Michael. Of course, the boats from Whitehorse would run every summer after the camp at Dawson was established.

A reindeer herd at St. Michael, 26 December 1913.

After I had been in Dawson many years, I went to the Wednesday evening meeting, as was my custom, and a friend stepped up to me and said she wanted to see me after the service, that I needed protection.

"Protection! What do you mean?"

"Never mind; wait until after the others go and I will tell you."

When we were alone she said, "You should go outside for a time, we think. You have not been feeling very well all winter, and have been working hard; and to go outside, to the States will do you good. Afterward, may be in a year or so, you can come back if you like." But I protested that

I did not have the money to make the trip then, but she told me not to bother about that, that my friends would advance the money and look after everything; so before I really knew what was happening I was on my way to the States.

I was just in time to catch the last boat before navigation closed on the Yukon. The ice had begun to run in the river, but the captain thought we could make Whitehorse all right. When we reached the Indian River, the ice began to come in so fast that we were stuck before we realized it. Our boat, the "Vidette," with Captain Harrington commanding, was pushed toward the shore and we grounded.

The men all jumped off and worked hard to push the boat off again. They built huge bonfires to melt the ice, as well as to illuminate the scene, for it was night when we jammed in the ice. We were a day's journey from Dawson, and had to send back for help. Ropes were tied to the boat and the men posted along the shore. They pulled and tugged, but the boat would not budge. Suddenly it began to lurch, which sent all the men sprawling into the snow, head first, their feet sticking into the air, and although it was quite a serious thing, there were great shouts of laughter at the grotesque shadows they made on the snow, their feet and arms waving wildly. They could not get the boat out of the ice, so the Government sent Indians to take us back to Dawson.

I stayed at a hotel for fourteen days, in Dawson, until the trail was in such condition that the stage could run. I started again, with my bags. Two young women who had come in to Dawson and established a fancy goods store, were also going outside, to see their mother in Seattle, and I was glad to have their company on the journey.

The coach carried the Royal mail and $30,000 in gold dust. We were loaded in tight and snug—even the driver was "loaded," if you will pardon the feeble remark. Evidently he had a flask of whiskey with him from which he continued to drink, for it was not long before we all realized that he was acting peculiarly. All at once, with a wild whoop, he drove the horses down a steep bank and tumbled us all out. We were not hurt much, as we landed in a deep snow bank. But as it was, many were cut and bruised. I had a gash over one eye.

One of the passengers who knew the road told us there was a road house about two miles on farther, so we picked up our belongings and started to walk. It was a sorry looking bunch of bandaged persons who ate dinner together that night at the road house. The driver, sobered by the accident, and with the help of others, stayed to unhitch the horses and to gather up the bags of mail and gold dust, and to pull the stage onto the road again. A new outfit of horses was secured, and the following morning we started out once more.

"Look here," I said to the driver, "don't you get drunk again. This is a pretty way to treat passengers. You stay sober the rest of the trip."

He was very sorry and promised not to drink anymore on the journey, and I felt that he meant it and was beginning to feel quite safe, when we were suddenly dumped down another bank. But it was not on account of the driver's being drunk this time. Evidently the tongue of the coach had been cracked in the first fall and it had not been noticed; for we found this time, after digging ourselves out of the snow, that the tongue was broken. So it was up to us to walk on to the next station. We all sat around the big heating stove in the dining room until morning. Then the coach was mended and after several more days on the road we arrived at White Horse.

Here we were comfortable at the White Horse Hotel, which had been built since the last time I passed through the town. The next morning we boarded the train for Skagway. But our trials were not all over yet. After we had been on the way three hours, our train broke down. It was a mixed train, with two freight cars loaded with copper, and the one in which the passengers rode being at the end. The freight cars were not strong enough to bear the weight of the ore, and broke down, blocking the track for hours.

The delay caused in clearing the track gave me an opportunity to cross the river and visit a fox farm that had been established there by a young German. He had about a hundred of the largest foxes I ever saw, and was raising them for their pelts. There were dozens of baby foxes, also of little minks. They would crawl up on his shoulders and run all over him, they were so tame.

They knew exactly when feeding time came, and if the butcher's boy from across the river did not get there on the minute with their meat, they would get wildly excited and snatch and growl at the man whom they had allowed to pet them a few moments before.

There were great yellow foxes—black, white, and mixed ones. The foxes I had seen in the United States looked like kittens compared with these fine big fellows, with their huge bushy tails.

And here I must remark about the wonderful protection of nature, whereby foxes in that country change their coats to white in the winter. The snow birds and the ptarmigan as well change their coats to white, which is a great protection to them in that land of snow and ice. Also the rabbits we saw on the trail coming out that time, were white, and quite tame. They would sit along the trail as the stage drove by; and as they sat in the snow it was hard to see anything but their little red eyes.

When I returned to the railroad station, I found that the cars had not yet been pushed off the track, so we were compelled to wait until the next day. I put two chairs together, in the crude waiting room, and tried to make a bed on them, but was doubled up like a jack-knife. The

S. S. Cutch in Skagway Harbor, circa 1910.

others distributed themselves on chairs and tried to get some rest.

The next morning we started once more. But all these delays had caused us to miss our boat, and there would not be another for a week. We at last found a small fishing boat which was bound for Seattle and we decided to go on it. We were all anxious to reach Seattle in time for Christmas Eve. The boat was so slow that we grew very impatient. The captain stopped at about every cannery along the way, to load fish. Once when a larger boat passed us, we waved and called to them to take us aboard. The captain did not seem to be in a hurry, he said, "Why, we are a nice, happy family, let's spend Christmas Eve together."

When we found that we would not be able to spend Christmas Eve in Seattle we decided to make the best of it. We found some boys among the crew who could play on different instruments and they furnished the music while the rest of us danced. There were women on the boat who had made some money, by cooking, clerking, and in other ways, and there wee trappers and miners aboard. Everyone was willing to contribute to a good time, and we made up a purse that delighted the musicians.

It was Christmas night when we landed in Seattle, and there was only one taxi at the dock. The two young girls who were with me and a young man who had been nice to our trio on the boat crowded into this car and started to find a hotel. It being a holiday the city was crowded, and all the hotels we visited were full up. We journeyed hopefully from one place to another, until the taxi broke down and we sat on the curb while the driver tried to fix it. But we were so cold and uncomfortable that we abandoned car and driver and continued our search on foot. It was two o'clock when we finally found accommodations.

I took the train to San Francisco the next day and found my daughter well, and my grandchildren all excited about the presents I had brought them.

"Mother, what do you want for dinner?" my daughter asked.

"Vegetables, just vegetables—but please don't give me any beans!"

"The Grand Opera Company is here; Caruso is singing in Cavalleria Rusticana; you should hear him," my daughter suggested.

I had been so hungry for fine music, that I went. It was glorious—wonderful! I "ate" music just as the starved miners on the Yukon stuffed themselves with eggs, or sugar. I went to the opera every night for six weeks, and truly it was a satisfying feast.

The next spring found me ready and anxious to go North again, with the other "birds of passage." I started so early that I had to wait in White Horse several weeks before the first boats could make the trip to Dawson. The hotel at White Horse was crowded, so I found a room next door. One day when the wind was blowing almost a hurricane, the woman in charge of the hotel cleaned some gloves with gasoline, in front of a hot stove. The stove exploded, and started a terrific fire, which resulted in her death. I heard the fire bell rung but paid no attention until my room began to fill with smoke and the flames were leaping just ouside my window. I frantically grabbed a few things and ran for my life. The next morning when I returned to my room, my bed, most of the stock of goods I had bought to take to Dawson, the furniture, were burned—except my Bible and a "little black book" which I prized very much, and which were on a shelf over my bed. These were scorched only a little bit but the contents were intact.

As I had not the money nor the opportunity to get another stock of goods that spring, I decided to stay in White Horse until I could work my way back to the States. Everyone was very kind to me, and soon I had all the sewing I could do. I stayed there a year, then went back to Skagway as I heard there was a lot of work there.

It was not until I arrived in Skagway that I found out what my Dawson friend had meant when she said I "needed protection," and why I had been sent back to the States. In Skagway I met an old friend from Dawson who was leaving for the outside but said she must first tell me something which had worried her greatly.

She clerked in a fruit store in Dawson and one day when she was in a small back room where the men used to play cards, she overheard two men talking and her attention was attracted when one of them mentioned my name, and said to the other "Look here you have got to do this for me. You know this claim she has, she can't handle it

Anna DeGraf, circa 1910.

any way. There is a skylight over her shop, she is under it most of the time. It would be the easiest thing in the world for you to drop something through that skylight, and nobody would ever know who did it. She would be dead in the morning, and that would be all there is to it."

She said while she had not told me, she had told some of my friends and that is why they sent me outside, to safety.

One of the interesting capable women of the pioneer days in the North is Mrs. Pullen, who was a very good friend to me. I stayed at her hotel the first few weeks I was in Skagway and had an opportunity to watch and admire her. She went through hardships aplenty, but was never daunted. If the stable boy got drunk and failed to show up, she would hitch up the horses, and take the bus to the train or boat and get the passengers. She had a farm at Dyea, which the hotel guests and others enjoyed visiting, to see how vegetables and fruits can be raised in that country; she also had some fine cows that furnished rich milk and cream for the hotel.

While I was there a drygoods merchant sent me all the work I could do. I moved to a little cabin near the hall where the dances and entertainments were held, and as I sat sewing in the evening, the girls going by to the dances would call to me, "Come on, Mother," and would bother me so I could not sew. Sometimes I would dress and go with them. I loved to dance and be with young people having a good time. I enjoyed the music, the bright lights, the pretty girls, their pretty clothes, and their manly escorts.

After a while when work grew slack, and I had saved some money, I moved on to Juneau, a little nearer my family in the States. This time I found it a prosperous northern town that had outgrown its mining-camp features. Most of those whom I knew in the early days had scattered, but I made new friends and spent two happy years in the Alaska capital. For by this time the capital had been moved from Sitka. Now we enjoyed electric lights, had telephones, a water system, good stores and hotels, and more comfortable houses. The boats ran more frequently bringing fruits and vegetables from Seattle, while some vegetables were grown near by.

Then news of the arrival of a great grand-daughter in San Francisco and a longing to see my family, caused me to say good-bye to the Northland, with regret at leaving my good friends and the democratic life of the frontier.

After visiting and resting a few months, I again became restless and this time sought work near at hand. I have been continuously employed sewing furs, as I learned to do it in the Yukon Territory. As I sit and stitch,

Anna DeGraf, San Francisco, 1924.

stitch, on the beautiful skins, some of which come from that far-away land, I live over the experiences I had on my travels of over thirty thousand miles in the Land of the Midnight Sun.

No word has ever come to me in all these years about my son, except the two reports I had of his having been seen in Juneau and at Forty Mile, but my hope is that someone who may read these words—even the boy himself—may send me a message and that I may see him again on this planet.

Anna DeGraf, Oakland, circa 1929.